Dinner at
BUCKINGHAM PALACE

Dinner at BUCKINGHAM PALACE

CHARLES OLIVER WORKED AT BUCKINGHAM PALACE FROM THE
REIGN OF QUEEN VICTORIA TO THAT OF THE PRESENT QUEEN.
BASED ON HIS DIARIES, THIS IS AN EXTRAORDINARY COLLECTION
OF PHOTOGRAPHS, RECIPES, ANECDOTES AND MENUS.

Published by Metro Publishing Ltd,
3 Bramber Court, 2 Bramber Road,
London W14 9PB, England

First published in hardback in 2003

ISBN 1 84358 062 4

British Library Cataloguing-in-Publication Data:

A catalogue record for this book is available from the British Library.

Design by ENVY

Printed in Spain by Bookprint

3 5 7 9 10 8 6 4 2

Papers used by Metro Publishing are natural, recyclable products made from wood grown in
sustainable forests. The manufacturing processes conform to the environmental regulations
of the country of origin.

Food pictures reproduced by kind permission of The Anthony Blake Photo Library.

Dinner at BUCKINGHAM PALACE

Edited and compiled by
Paul Fishman and Fiorella Busoni.

With additional material by
*Paul Fishman, Fiorella Busoni, Nika Hazelton,
and Richard Warwick.*

CONTENTS

Introduction

Dinner at Buckingham Palace is a unique collection of authentic recipes from the royal cookery books. It is also a historic reflection of the culinary habits of the royal household, from Victoria to Elizabeth II. Based on the diaries and personal recollections of Charles Oliver, a servant who lived and worked for most of his life within the palace, the book includes over 190 recipes, to suit family and intimate gatherings or for such auspicious and grand occasions as banquets. Dinner at Buckingham Palace provides a fascinating insight into royal food, serving procedures, personal preferences, kitchens, dining rooms and menu books.

REQUIRED SKILLS: A LARGE STAFF (OPTIONAL)

In many cookery books dealing with food in noble houses, the recipes are written by chefs for other chefs, or by gracious ladies and gentlemen for other gracious ladies and gentlemen. In the first case, the recipes are very technical and generally cater for enormous quantities – the way chefs are apt to cook. In the second case, the recipes are charmingly written but extremely vague, making it apparent that the author never actually cooked them but is merely reproducing remarks gathered from professionals who express themselves in chefs' language. Neither is really suitable for the home kitchen, requiring either a scaling down or a certain amount of experimentation until the intended results are achieved. This book (with a few exceptions) contains recipes that have been adapted and worked out for the home kitchen and the home cook, using readily available ingredients. Of course, some of the culinary terms,

measurements and recipes are a little recherché. These are explained fully in the Glossary.

While not impossible, it would be simply too impractical to re-create the larger and more extravagant menus today. The state dinners given in 1841, when the young Victoria had been Queen for only four years, boggle the mind. It would be a serious task to create the plethora of complicated meals masked with extravagant sauces, the colourful fish courses and the architectural sweets. The main difficulty would be assembling a large enough kitchen staff that had the necessary techniques; the kind of staff taken for granted in the times of Victoria and Edward VII, when young men and women served long, arduous years as apprentices to their trade. Dinners such as these require not only accomplished chefs but a staff where even the humblest vegetable parer accepts

the concept of very ornate food and works towards this end. Nowadays few chefs, sous-chefs and kitchen personnel could equal the skills of their Victorian and Edwardian counterparts. For example, how many of them know – or care to know – how to make a crystal-clear aspic, the base for so many decorative cold dishes? How many take the trouble to make a proper espagnole as a base for other sauces? How many pastry chefs or cooks know how to spin or mould sugar into fairy-tale centrepieces? And of course, the dozens of ornate culinary creations that comprised the Victorian and Edwardian state dinners are far removed from present-day eating habits.

CHARLES OLIVER

'Charlie' Oliver was the son of a royal servant who served at Balmoral at the end of the 19th century, during the reign of Queen Victoria. When Charles was born they continued to live within the royal household and, as young Charlie grew up, like his father he became part of the entourage of employees who served and tended the monarchy and their guests. It was practically inevitable that the child of a servant should follow in his or her parents' footsteps, as to serve the monarchy was considered a great honour. Charles continued to work for the royal household for most of his life but at the outbreak of World War I he left to join the army and fight for his country. Caught in the historic battle at Gallipoli, he was gravely wounded, but somehow managed to survive, with only one lung and permanent partial paralysis. After his recovery he returned to royal service and was appointed to the personal staff of the Prince of Wales, now serving under King George V and Queen Mary.

It was said that his diligence and endless good humour endeared him to the staff and to the King and Queen and he was in many ways quite a remarkable character. He was known at Buckingham Palace where he was employed for many years, at Windsor Castle where he worked under the rule of housekeeper Alice Bruce, and at Balmoral. As a result of his injuries he was left with a serious speech impediment but this managed to bring him even closer to the royal family circle, for 'Bertie' (King George VI) also stammered. Charles Oliver later on returned to employment at the Palace and continued to work under the authority of Sir Piers Leigh, Master of the Household, whose right-hand man he later became.

He remained throughout his life a bachelor but devoted much of his time when not serving King, Queen and country to acquiring both a taste and knowledge of good food. He was particularly fascinated by the royal kitchens, keeping endless notes recording every detail, and over a period of many years he gradually amassed a considerable collection of royal recipes and menus, of which he was extremely proud. He also lovingly and respectfully hoarded a treasure of many anecdotes relating to the serving of these dishes, recording state social event souvenirs, royal tastes and entertaining preferences, to make his own unique and very individual commentary.

Charlie suggested that the wealth of material he had gathered over the years should be compiled into what he described as 'a cookbook with a difference'. He made only one stipulation: that it should not be published until after his death.

Throughout his life he remained very close to those who continued to live and work at the Palace, and after retiring Charlie still regularly returned to visit, as he lived nearby in a basement apartment in Bucking Gate. Despite his age and his physical handicaps he served as a London borough councillor and was employed as a guide at the Houses of Parliament and Westminster Abbey. Charles Oliver died in 1965.

A few years later in 1968, through a contact at the palace, the contents of his diaries and collections were brought to the attention of English author Jack Fishman who was a former editor of one of the country's national newspapers. Having worked as a professional journalist for a considerable time, Fishman had acquired many political and royal contacts. Since departing the newspaper he had established himself as a successful author, including biographies

on Bogart, Stalin and notably the internationally acclaimed *My Darling Clementine*, the biography of Lady Churchill.

Recognizing the unique content and historic value of Charles Oliver's diaries, Jack Fishman made various attempts to get them published but for many years most of the material remained literally buried in his attic. The original manuscript for this book was later discovered after Fishman's own death in 1997.

Among the vast collection of papers, documents and photographs that he had collected, there were some unpublished personal, charming family photos of the King and Queen with their young children. Some of these had been given to Fishman by Lord Mountbatten who along with other members of the royal family had fondly admired the biography of Lady Churchill. Mountbatten was interested in the possibility of Fishman writing his own biography, but owing to his sudden death the book did not come to fruition.

These photographs have now been included within this book, along with other rare royal photos found in Fishman's collection.

A Brief History of Royal Cooking

The Tudor and Elizabethan monarchs enjoyed enormous and extravagant feasts, as did the high-living aristocracy of succeeding centuries, who were close enough to the royal court to accept its standards even in non-royal entertainment. In 1746 the Earl of Warwick held a banquet for more than 6,000 people, where a great marble basin was filled with a punch made from 25,000 lemons, 80 pints of lemon juice, 4 large barrels of water, 1,003 hundredweights of sugar, 300 biscuits and 5 lb of nutmeg. They were obviously thirsty!

A great change in the nature and quality of English food took place in the early part of the nineteenth century. After the French Revolution and the Napoleonic Wars many French chefs were left without noble houses to employ them and came over to England to put their enduring stamp on English cooking. French, or at least Frenchified, food became the most desirable cuisine and dishes were given French names regardless of their origins; a practice that still exists to the present day. The introduction of French kitchen techniques also led to a lessening of the English appetite. Dumplings became quenelles, fish was transformed into soufflés, meat was enhanced with sauces, socles of rice or pastry held composed salads and other dishes, and desserts became rich and a far cry from the homey English pie. Even typically English foods, notably game, were cooked in a more imaginative manner.

Venison and game birds were, from the Middle Ages onward, very much British favourites, and their peak of consumption was reached during Victorian and Edwardian times.

The chef who had the greatest influence on this development was Antonin Careme (1784–1833), one of the master chefs of all times and creator of immensely elaborate confectionary, as depicted in his drawings – they have to be seen to be believed. Widely regarded as the founder of haute cuisine, Careme was chef to Talleyrand, Tsar Alexander I and England's George IV, who enjoyed vast quantities of high-quality food.

VICTORIAN EXTRAVAGANCE

Royal eating habits during the reigns of Queen Victoria and King Edward VII followed a similarly lavish approach to their predecessors.

At least five different courses were served for the royal breakfast. Bacon and eggs, bloaters, chickens, chops, cutlets, sausages, steaks and woodcocks, were just some of the dishes on offer. The bacon, invariably streaky, was cut in rashers a quarter of an inch thick, and eggs would be served at a moment's notice in a variety of ways, including boiled, fried, coddled, en cocotte, scrambled or as an omelette.

Despite such huge breakfasts, the royal household was apparently hungry again by lunchtime, when meals of eight or ten courses were the order of the day. And by dinnertime they were ready for more – again to the tune of eight or ten courses!

The royal supper was undoubtedly the most elaborate meal of the day. It was customary to serve both thick and clear soups, as well as fish either plainly cooked or prepared according to elaborate recipes requiring complicated sauces and flamboyant dressing. There would also be two entrées, two varieties of roast meat, chicken or quail, collettes of game, sweetbreads, two desserts, two savouries and at least two kinds of water ices to prepare overburdened royal stomachs for the next course. Notably there is no reference to hors d'oeuvres, which most likely originated in Russia, where people ate highly flavoured tidbits called zakuski with a drink of vodka before settling down to dinner. English restaurants adopted the custom at the end of the nineteenth century because it kept the guests happy while dinner was cooked, and English private houses duly followed suit.

The great gas and charcoal stoves and spits would daily cook something like 300 lb of meat, 30 or more chickens, and numerous pheasants, partridges and quails. If necessary, a whole bullock weighing about 150 lb could be cooked on a giant spit, with a small army of chefs and kitchen assistants on hand to keep it continually basted. Another outsized dish, which was a great favourite of Queen Victoria's, was known as Raized Pie. It was prepared by stuffing a good plump turkey with an equally plump chicken, itself stuffed with an ample pheasant that had been stuffed with a healthy-sized woodcock! The whole lot was then placed in an enormous pie dish, roofed over with pastry and baked until it was fit for a queen. And just in case anybody ever felt hungry after consuming one of the huge luncheons or dinners, there were always side tables set out with cold chickens, tongues, rounds of beef, partridges and pheasants in season, and salads.

This was high living, of course. Middle-class families ate simple meals, though not quite as simple as those of today's middle-class families, while the poor consumed small quantities of cheap foods, such as fish and chips, sausage rolls, bread and jam – and very often they didn't eat at all. There was widespread hunger in Victorian times and prostitution was rampant, largely due to the lack of food. It was small wonder that the impoverished would congregate in the street outside the royal kitchens, and each day many went away satisfied with a liberal helping of leftovers from the royal table.

Queen Victoria herself was a frugal eater and showed little interest in food — for breakfast she ate only an egg, served in a gold eggcup with a gold spoon. Nevertheless, as can be seen from her menus at the end of this book, as the head of an empire she had to set an imperial table. One particular course she insisted should be available for lunch was a dish of curry and rice, served with considerable ceremony by two Indian servants resplendent in uniforms of blue and gold. Victoria took pride in being empress of India and loved to surround herself with vividly attired Indian footmen and waiters. It could reasonably be supposed that it was as much the ceremony of the serving as it was the tastiness of the dish itself that prompted her to order it daily.

In the closing years of her reign, Victoria had a residential staff of more than a hundred people at Windsor and a kitchen staff of 45, during which time the head chef was a Frenchman, Monsieur Menager. For state celebrations even more staff were employed — for the Diamond Jubilee in 1897, 24 extra chefs were brought in to prepare the food, which took several days.

Although meals during the reign of Edward VII were simpler than during Victoria's time, they still seem enormous by today's standards. Unlike his mother, the King liked to eat. A typical lunch for six might include cold pheasant, a couple of partridges, two hot roast fowls, and hot beefsteaks. Dinner always featured a choice of at least two soups, whole salmons and turbots, vast saddles of mutton and sirloins of beef, roast turkeys, several kinds of game such as woodcocks, plovers and snipe, a large array of vegetables, perhaps some deviled herring and cream cheese, an assortment of pastries, and enormous Stilton and Cheshire cheeses. The whole was accompanied by a profusion of wines followed by nuts and preserved fruits, then Madeira, port or sherry.

During visits to the theatre or opera, Edward would insist on a one-hour interval so that he could fully appreciate his supper, served in the royal box. The six royal hampers packed for such occasions contained such items as cold clear soup, lobster mayonnaise, cold trout, plovers' eggs, cold duck, chicken, lamb cutlets, ham and tongue, a selection of sandwiches, a choice of some four desserts and Parisian pastries. Gold plate was taken along as well to remind the King that it was a royal meal, even if it came from hampers.

POST-WAR MODERATION

The fantastic feeding habits in the royal palace, castles and country houses during Victorian and Edwardian days changed abruptly with the First World War. Eating traditions had been slowly transforming since King George V ascended the throne, as he had the appetite of a professional sailor rather than a social gourmet, and Queen Mary had insisted on rationing in the palace even before the nation had been subjected to it. She would let no member of the family eat more than two courses for breakfast and at her insistence the royal chefs became skilled at contriving mock meat cutlets from mutton purée. Although Mary was undoubtedly one of the greatest connoisseurs of food the palace has known, she set a steadfast example in changing and simplifying the royal eating habits. George V, meanwhile, prohibited the drinking of wine or indeed any alcohol as long as the war lasted, and guests at his table were offered a concoction amounting to little more than sugar boiled in a lot of water. The King himself took to drinking a thin soup for elevenses, nearly always had mashed potatoes instead of anything fancy, and seemed never to tire of apple dumplings

for dessert. On the few occasions George V entertained on any scale at the palace during the war, no meat was served either at luncheon or dinner. The final death knell of the old days of gluttony and waste was sounded in 1932 when a big cut was made in court expenditure and the royal household staff was greatly reduced, with many older servants being pensioned off.

During the reign of King George VI, in the days soon after the war when food was scarce, the palace faithfully observed rationing and similar restrictions confronting other families. On one occasion the King and Queen were

holding a small private dinner party, and the kitchen had been instructed accordingly. Unfortunately, the head chef was off duty for the night and a deputy had been put in charge of the meal. Still more unfortunately, an old army buddy of the deputy chef had called by earlier that evening to renew his acquaintance and there had been a certain amount of celebrating, which resulted in the chef being unfit to cook the King's dinner. Unaware of his limitations, the chef proceeded to cook the meal – and burnt it beyond hope of revival or disguise. An ashen-faced chef announced the terrible news to a footman, who passed it onto a page, who then had the misfortune to have to relay it to the King. The poor chef had fully expected to be escorted to the Tower, particularly as, due to current circumstances, the royal cupboard was literally bare, with absolutely nothing to replace the incinerated meal. The King reacted swiftly and, for all the fears below stairs, sympathetically. However, he did not attempt to hide his annoyance and issued an immediate instruction to send out to the nearest hotel for four dinners. Half an hour later dinner duly arrived, rushed to the palace in heated containers by breathless kitchen staff. Nothing more was said about the incident. The King

even forgave the deputy chef, who remained employed in the palace kitchens for many years. Since the early twentieth century, the royal attitude to food and diet has dramatically changed, with preference towards more ordinary food. When Mrs Roosevelt served George VI and Queen Elizabeth hot dogs as typical American fare, the royal couple was amused. (It does not bear thinking what the King's grandfather, Edward VII, would have said.)

And when the Queen was married in 1947, her wedding breakfast consisted only of four separate courses, and it was all over in twenty minutes.

In modest contrast with the lavish royal eating of yesteryear, a straight-forward steak-and-kidney pudding is today a favourite of Prince Philip. When the Monday Club, the successor to the Thursday Club, held its inaugural dinner at a Knightsbridge restaurant, Prince Philip requested that steak and kidney should be the principal dish. The simple menu for the occasion comprised hors d'oeuvres, pudding and asparagus from the gardens of Windsor Castle. The Duke also insisted on vodka glasses so that the vodka chasers for the strong Australian lager could be drunk in the Russian manner – in one gulp.

Eggs

BREAKFAST IS SERVED

The Queen normally rises soon after 8 a.m. and has breakfast with her husband in the Green Tea Room at 9 a.m. On the rare occasions that she breakfasts in bed, a tray is taken up to the first-floor royal suite by the Queen's Footman, who then passes the tray to her maid, officially known as the Queen's Dresser. Members of the royal family who frequently enjoyed taking breakfast in bed were Princess Margaret, the Earl of Snowdon and the Queen Mother.

The Queen's customary breakfast is fried egg and bacon, or scrambled egg, served with tea (never coffee) and fresh, chilled orange juice, a jug of which is always on the table. The Queen Mother was also a great fan of fresh orange juice, and sometimes confined herself to several glasses for her breakfast.

If the Queen prefers to take breakfast in one of the palace's dining rooms, the footmen take in what are known in the silver pantry as the 'aircraft carriers', so called because of their likeness in shape to the flight deck of an aircraft carrier. The rectangular silver dishes each have a cavity underneath to hold hot water, which enables the dish to stay hot. In particular, they are used for taking omelettes or scrambled eggs to the table.

Breakfast is often accompanied by the muted sound of bagpipes played by the Queen's piper, who traditionally plays beneath her window at this time — whatever the weather. After breakfast, the Queen's footman has what is known in the palace as a 'waiting period'. If the Queen is still in the palace, the waiting will almost certainly be interrupted by elevenses, when orange juice or tea and biscuits are served using the white-bone china tea service decorated with dainty blue flowers. The next occasion footmen are required to attend the royal table is lunch at 1 p.m. If so, it will be listed in the kitchen as 'Lunch-Royal for 2 (Waited)'; otherwise it will be shown as 'All-in'.

When the royal children were younger their breakfast was often served in the palace nursery on the third floor above the royal suite.

A PASSION FOR EGGS

The present Queen has always favoured the simple dish of eggs for breakfast and has them served in a variety of ways. Scrambled and fried are her preferences, but she also enjoys omelettes, poached eggs (normally served with fried bread croûtons), eggs en cocotte à la crème, plat au lard, frits à la française, and just plain boiled. In fact Her Majesty is a bit of a specialist when it comes to eggs, and is one of the many who insist that, whatever nutrition experts may say, a brown egg tastes better. She discovered a farm at Windsor, where hens produce eggs of an abnormal size and have an extra-special taste.

Eggs are also family favourites at the palace. Prince Charles is a fan of boiled egg, or sometimes baked, while Prince Philip prefers omelettes to any other egg dish — and even insists on cooking them himself in his glass-covered electric frying pan.

The Queen has a soft spot for sausages, too, and has frequently been known to

choose sausages in preference to suggested dishes. Other typical breakfast suggestions listed in the royal menu book are: scrambled eggs and bacon; chipolatas; poached eggs and bacon; fish cakes; omelette and bacon; smoked haddock; kippers; sauté kidney; cold ham; and a decidedly 'untypical' variation – oeufs en cocotte à la crème with minced chicken.

Omelette aux Fines Herbes

(Serves two people)

3-4 eggs
1 tablespoon water
butter
seasoning
1 dessertspoon (each)
    finely chopped parsley,
chives, chervil and
    tarragon

Whisk the eggs and water while feeding in the chopped herbs and seasoning. Place a thick-bottomed omelette pan on strong heat and when it is very hot drop in a knob of butter. As it froths tip the pan from side to side so that it becomes coated all over with butter. Now pour in the egg mixture, continuing to tilt the pan so that the liquid fills it evenly. As the omelette quickly cooks give the pan regular, sharp jolts to settle the mixture and stroke with a fork in from the sides to the centre. Ease the edges of the stiffening omelette with a thin, flat blade so that liquid on top can run underneath. When the top of the omelette is of a consistency resembling scrambled egg, and the underside has formed a golden-brown skin, fold the omelette in half and drop another knob of butter into the pan. Gently lift the omelette to let the hot butter run underneath to crisp and brown the undersurface, which happens very quickly. As soon as this is done, turn the omelette out on to a hot dish and eat at once.

Oeufs Plat Chasseur

For the chasseur sauce:

¾ lb mushrooms

butter

1 tablespoon chopped
    shallots

1 tablespoon flour

½ cup white wine

1 cup consommé or
    white stock

1 teaspoon tomato purée

1 tablespoon chopped
    parsley, chervil and
    tarragon

Liberally butter individual baking dishes and carefully break 2 eggs into each dish. Put the dishes in a baking tin containing an inch or two of hot water and bake in a fairly hot oven (400°F/Gas 6) until the egg whites are firm. Garnish the eggs with sautéed chicken livers, surround with chasseur sauce and sprinkle with chopped parsley.

TO MAKE THE CHASSEUR SAUCE:

Chop the mushrooms into a pan and toss them in butter with the chopped shallots. Remove the mushrooms when cooked, then add the flour to the butter and cook gently until golden. Dilute with the white wine and stir in the consommé or white stock and the tomato purée. Boil the mixture down, then add back the mushrooms.

At the last moment, add 2 tablespoons of butter and the chopped parsley, chervil and tarragon.

Omelette and Bacon

Allow 2 eggs per person. Beat or whisk the eggs in a basin, and for each lot of eggs add a good pinch of salt and pepper and 1 tablespoon of water. Drop a generous knob of butter into an omelette pan and heat until it becomes liquid, tilting the pan to run a film of butter all over the surface. Now pour in the eggs.

Let the mixture cook for about 1 minute over a high heat to set the bottom of the omelette, then loosen the mixture around the sides of the pan. Cook rapidly, tipping the pan from all angles so that any liquid mixture flows underneath. When the omelette is set, slip a slice or palette knife under the omelette and fold it away from the handle. Garnish with parsley and serve on hot plates with bacon, which has been grilling in the meantime.

Bouchées d'Oeufs

These are puff-pastry patties, baked unfilled and afterwards filled or garnished with hard-boiled egg bound with hot velouté, allemande or béchamel sauce or cream.

TO MAKE THE PATTIES:
First, roll out the puff pastry six times. Roll it out for a seventh time to a thickness of about ¼ inch. Using a round, fluted pastry-cutter cut out circlets 2 inches in diameter — as many as you need patties. Set out the circlets, turning them on a just-moistened metal tray. Brush the circlets with egg, then mark out the lids with a pastry-cutter 1 ¼ inches in diameter, taking care not to cut right through. Bake the patties in a hot oven, then remove the lids and scoop out the soft interior from the lower half.

The patties should be filled or garnished at the very last moment and should be put into the oven for 20 seconds or so just before filling. If you can add the filling the minute they come out of the oven, so much the better, as it makes a tremendous difference to the flavour.

THE MENU BOOKS

Each day the Queen selects menus from a list of suggestions written by the royal chef, presented in a red leather-bound book stamped in gold with the words 'Menu Royal'.

The menu book is usually taken to the Queen in her private suite, or soon after she arrives in her office, normally at around 10 a.m. The office, originally known as the Tapestry Room, is on the first floor looking out at the lawn that stretches to the lake. There, the Queen marks in pencil her final selection, striking out dishes she doesn't want and writing in alternatives. This is copied as a notice for the several departments of the kitchen concerned with providing the royal meals. The Menu Royal is then put in a safe place in readiness for the head chef to make suggestions for the following morning.

When a menu book is full, it is sent to the palace library, where scores of these leather-bound volumes, some red, some black, are filed. With the pencilled-in notes and suggestions of a succession of Queens of England, they form a unique record of the eating habits and fancies of many generations of British royalty. They also record the special dishes served for visitors, including foreign royalty and statesmen, whose names are written into the book if they have dined privately with the monarch.

Fried Egg and Bacon

Heat fat in a frying pan until hot and just beginning to smoke. Then break each egg into a cup before dropping it into the hot fat. Cook the egg gently until it is set, basting it with hot fat to cook it on top as well as underneath. Loosen the egg with a slice and lift out carefully.

Cut the rind and any hard edges off the bacon, and snip the fat at intervals to prevent the rasher curling. Lay the rashers flat in the pan and cook gently at first to melt the fat. Then quickly increase the heat and cook both sides.

To grill the bacon, prepare the rashers as before and cook under a hot grill, turning frequently.

Oeufs Brouillés Meyerbeer

Scramble and cook as many eggs as required and garnish with grilled lamb kidney. Serve on a hot dish surrounded with a circle of Périgueux sauce.

TO MAKE THE SAUCE:
Gently cook 2 tablespoons of diced raw truffles in butter, season with salt and pepper, and drain. Add 1 tablespoon of Madeira to the juices and stir in 1 cup of concentrated, thickened brown stock. Simmer for 2 or 3 minutes, then strain. Return the truffles back to the sauce, add 2 tablespoons of Madeira and keep hot without allowing it to boil.

Omelette aux Tomates

Break 2 eggs per person into a large basin and for each lot of eggs add a tablespoon of water. Now add a good pinch of salt and pepper and beat or whisk thoroughly. Do not attempt to cook more than 4 eggs in a 6-inch pan because it will take too long and the omelette will become leathery.

Drop a knob of butter into an omelette pan (preferably), heat until it is faintly smoking and run it round the whole inside of the pan. Now pour in the eggs and leave for about 1 minute over a high heat. When the bottom of the omelette has set, loosen from the sides of the pan with a slice and cook rapidly, tipping the pan from side to side to ensure that the liquid egg flows underneath and cooks quickly. When the omelette has just set, spread the tomato filling over the surface and, using a palette knife underneath, fold the omelette away from the handle. Serve immediately on hot plates.

TO MAKE THE TOMATO FILLING:
Plunge the tomatoes in boiling water, then remove the skin, pith and all the hard parts. Dice and simmer in butter, until tender, then season well and keep warm until required.

Scrambled Egg

Allow 2 eggs per person. Beat the eggs with fresh milk, allowing about 1 tablespoonful of milk to each lot of eggs. Heat a generous knob of butter in a saucepan and pour in the eggs. Cook over a good heat, continually stirring from the bottom until the mixture starts to thicken. Reduce the heat to very low and continue cooking until the required consistency has been attained (some people like their scrambled eggs almost runny, others prefer them stiff). Serve on freshly made and well-buttered hot toast, garnished with a small sprig of parsley.

THE QUEEN'S KITCHEN

Soon after the Queen came to the throne she set about modernizing the kitchens that provide food for the royal table in Buckingham Palace. The original kitchens are vast, inconvenient rooms beneath the great state ball and supper rooms in the far south-west corner of the palace, and are really only used for state banquets and balls when there are hundreds of guests to be catered for.

The Queen's kitchens are neither large nor elaborate by today's general standards, but an adaptation of old, somewhat hastily constructed royal kitchens, augmented with more modern equipment among old fittings. The kitchens are divided into two rooms, one for preparing and the other for cooking. A notable feature is the splendid array of shining bowls and utensils, all made from solid copper. The presence of so much glowing copper in the royal kitchens is mainly the Queen's idea, although former royal cook Ronald Aubrey was in complete agreement when it came to assessing their practicability as well as appearance.

Much the same thing has been done at Windsor Castle. Instead of the great medieval kitchens, with their need for vast staff and unlimited fuel when the royal family are in residence, the Queen had a small kitchen constructed nearer her suite in the Queen's Tower. The kitchen is in what used to be known as the Coffee Room – a room whose sole use was to provide coffee for the monarch and his family and guests. Before the Queen had the small kitchen constructed, a truly hot meal rarely reached the royal table, as all the food had to be brought by mobile hot-plate through a labyrinth of cold stone passages.

When the Queen is entertaining a large number of guests, such as the Ascot party at Windsor, the vast old kitchens over by the north wing are used.

Oeufs en Cocotte à la Crème with Minced Chicken

Into each cocotte (a small, fireproof earthenware dish) pour 1 tablespoon of boiling cream then carefully break 1 egg, putting a small nut of butter on the yolk.

Stand the cocottes in a pan of hot water and bake in the oven. When the eggs are cooked, garnish with sautéed minced chicken and serve.

Oeufs Farcis à la Chimay

Boil 6 good-sized eggs until hard and cut them in half lengthways. Rub the yolks through a sieve and mix with an equal amount of finely chopped cooked mushrooms, 1 ½ tablespoons of soft butter, 2 tablespoons of Mornay sauce, ½ teaspoon of salt and a little pepper. Press this mixture carefully into the halved whites and heap it up.

Spread an even layer of Mornay sauce into a shallow baking dish, then place the stuffed eggs on top. Cover the eggs with sufficient Mornay sauce to coat each one well. Sprinkle with grated Parmesan cheese and brown under the grill or in a preheated, very hot oven.

TO MAKE THE MORNAY SAUCE:
Grate 1 oz each of Parmesan and Gruyère cheese. Stir the grated cheese into a pint of béchamel sauce over a moderate heat. Finally stir in 2 ½ oz of fresh butter a few moments before serving.

Omelette Argenteuil

Make and cook the omelette in the usual way. Before folding it, however, fill it with 3 tablespoons of asparagus tips cooked in butter. Arrange 1 tablespoon of asparagus tips on top of the omelette and surround with a ring of cream sauce.

TO MAKE THE CREAM SAUCE:

To 1 cup of béchamel sauce add ½ cup of cream and cook until reduced by a third. Remove from the heat and add 3 tablespoons of butter and 4 tablespoons of cream. Strain and pour round the omelette.

Eggs à la Tripe

Boil 8 eggs until hard, then immerse them in cold water for 3 minutes. Peel off the shells, cut the eggs into fairly thick slices, then put them into a stew pan. Next, slice 3 small onions, separating the rings, then parboil them in water before boiling in white broth. Drain them into a sieve, then add them to the eggs. Add 2 ragoût-spoonfuls of good béchamel sauce, as much garlic as can be held on the point of a knife, a pinch of mignonette-pepper, a little nutmeg and the juice of 1 lemon. Toss the mixture together over the stove and, when the eggs are quite hot, dish them up in a conical shape. Garnish with croûtons or fleurons and serve.

Eggs au Gratin

Boil the eggs until hard, then immerse them in cold water before taking off the shells. Cut them into slices and set them aside on a plate. Next put a large ragoût-spoonful of white sauce into a stewpan and boil. When it is sufficiently reduced, add 2 oz of grated Parmesan cheese, a small pat of butter, a little nutmeg, a pinch of mignonette-pepper, the yolks of 4 eggs, and the juice of ½ lemon. Stir the mixture quickly over the stove until it begins to thicken, then with-draw it from the heat. Place the eggs into a dish in close, circular rows and spread some of the mixture between each layer to create a dome shape. Pour the remainder of the sauce over the surface, scatter some fried breadcrumbs mixed with grated Parmesan cheese over the top, and put some fried bread croûtons or fleurons round the base. Transfer the dish to the oven and bake, or gratinate, for about 10 minutes, then serve.

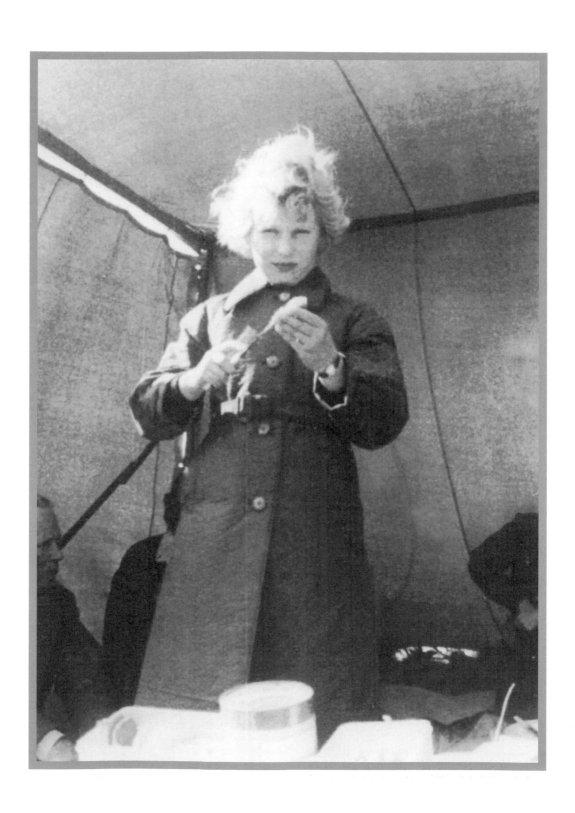

Tea

EVERYTHING STOPS FOR TEA

*T*eatime is one of the Queen's most favourite meals as inevitably, due to state engagements and other commitments, she rarely gets the opportunity to eat with her family at home, within the privacy of the palace dining room.

When her children were younger, teatime was the main family meal, with only the occasional guest or friend in attendance. The children would normally have their tea in the royal nursery half an hour before the grown-ups, at 4.30 p.m., which was followed by supper at 7 p.m. During this time a frequent visitor was Madame Eugene Untermyer, the Queen's governess for ten years. She was very much adored by the Queen, who would sometimes visit her flat in Chelsea to take tea with her. Unlike other guests, Madame Untermyer would always greet the Queen with a kiss on the cheek, instead of the more formal curtsy.

The Queen loves a cup of tea. This was never more evident than when she called at the home of the Pakistani Minister one morning during a visit to Stockholm. Her host's wife, an English woman, provided champagne and sherry for the occasion but the Queen did not seem too keen. Spotting a silver teapot on a side table, she indicated that tea would be her preference, confiding to her hostess, 'We are nearly always offered something alcoholic when we visit people in the morning, you know, but what I really do like is a nice cup of tea.' Like her husband and her mother, the Queen considers that gleaming silver makes a drink taste better, which is why her tea table is so elegantly furnished with a solid silver teapot, cream jug and sugar basin.

The ritual of English teatime was perfected by Queen Mary, for whom it was a treasured time of day. Everything had to ready by 4.00 p.m. prompt. Sandwiches, cakes and biscuits were invitingly set out on gleaming silver dishes. The teapot, hot-water jug, cream jug and sugar bowl were the same antique silver service that had been the favourite of Queen Victoria, while the cups, saucers and plates were the select choice of Queen Mary. At precisely 4.30 p.m. a footman would wheel in a trolley, immediately followed by another footman with a trolley carrying a spirit stove on which sat a kettle filled with preheated water. At this point Queen Mary would take over the proceedings and meticulously measure out level teaspoons of her favourite Indian tea from a jade tea caddy she kept locked in a cupboard. She added one teaspoon for each person and then 'one for the pot', which had already been warmed, of course. After pouring in the water, she would allow precisely three minutes for the tea to brew before it was ready to pour.

Nowadays, tea is invariably served in the beautiful bow-windowed Queen's Sitting Room, where the Queen and Prince Philip like to relax in comfortable tub armchairs and watch television as they sip their hot beverages. Official teas, when there are a number of guests present, are served in the Green Tea Room and are always attended by royal footman and butlers, who offer plates of sandwiches and cakes and, of course, tea. The tables are covered with a crisp white damask cloth, embroidered in the centre with the royal coat of arms, under which are the words 'Honi soit qui mal y pense', and decorated with English roses, Scottish thistles and Welsh daffodils.

Matching napkins are similarly embroidered. Often a delicate pink china tea-set known as 'Louis' is used for these occasions, which is rimmed with gold leaf and has a white band on the inside of the cup handles.

When the Queen is at Windsor, weather permitting, she likes to take both breakfast and tea beneath a striped awning on the terrace immediately beside the Queen's Tower. At other times, for example when guests are present, it is served in the handsome, oak-panelled drawing room, known as the Oak Dining Room. The Balmoral drawing room has a particularly spectacular view out across the immediate valley of the River Dee, with its backdrop of mountains and forest.

Rich Fruit Cake

6-8 eggs
12 oz flour
10 oz margarine
6 oz mixed peel
1 lb currants
8 oz raisins
1 lb sultanas
4 oz glacé cherries
4 oz blanched almonds
10 oz castor sugar
1 lemon
2 teaspoons mixed spice
pinch salt
little milk

Thoroughly clean the fruit, then chop the almonds, cherries and mixed peel. Ensure that the margarine is malleable, but not oversoft. Cream it together with the sugar until light and soft. Next, break the eggs separately into a basin, gently beating each one. Then transfer them, one after the other, into the creamed mixture, beating them thoroughly as you do so. The resultant texture should be light and fluffy. Sieve the dry ingredients into a bowl, add the fruit and grated lemon rind, and carefully fold into the mixture. Add a squeeze of lemon juice and a little milk, continuing to mix until the cake mixture is of an even consistency. Transfer it to a lined 9-inch tin and bake for about 5 hours, first at 350° F/Gas 4, then reducing to 300° F/Gas 2.

Ginger Cake

6 oz black treacle or
    golden syrup
4 oz brown sugar
2 eggs
5 oz butter
7 oz flour
1 teaspoon grated lemon rind
few pieces chopped ginger
1 tablespoon water

First, mix together well all the dry ingredients. Melt the butter and sugar and stir in the treacle and water. Now pour the liquid on to the dry mixture and beat well. Next, thoroughly beat in the eggs and lemon rind. Pour the mixture into a well-lined baking tin and bake (325° F/Gas 3) for 1 hour, or a little more as required. Allow the cake to cool before removing it from the tin.

Sandwiches Jambon et Langue

Use only really fresh bread, and ham and tongue that have been freshly sliced. After placing thin slices of the meat in the sandwiches, trim neatly and press the top and bottom layers of bread firmly together to make certain the sandwiches do not come apart.

A plate of sandwiches may not look especially exciting on its own, but garnishes can make a lot of difference. As well as the conventional parsley, try halved tomatoes, watercress, prawns, cocktail onions or radish flowers.

Mincemeat Puffs

Bake as many small vol au-vents as required. Be sure to have mincemeat ready to fill the vol-au-vents while still piping hot. Add generous portions of fresh cream and serve immediately if possible.

Queen's Cakes

2 oz sultanas
4 oz castor sugar
2 eggs
½ teaspoon baking powder
4 oz flour
4 oz margarine
little milk

Brush the insides of the cake tins with melted lard. Cream the margarine and sugar together, then thoroughly beat in the eggs. Sift the flour and baking powder and add to the creamed mixture, introducing the sultanas at the same time. Add sufficient milk to give a soft consistency and half-fill the tins with mixture. Now bake in a moderate oven (350°F/Gas 4) for about 20 minutes until the cakes are golden.

Scones

8 oz flour
2 oz margarine
2 oz sugar
2 oz currants
1 egg for mixing
small amount of milk (optional)
1 teaspoon of cream of tartar
¼ teaspoon of salt
½ teaspoon bicarbonate of soda
egg to glaze

Make a soft dough by mixing the ingredients, including the egg (and a little milk if necessary). Place on a lightly floured board and gently roll or pat out the dough to a thickness of about ¼-1 inch. Using a small plain cutter, cut out the scones and put them in a greased tin, making sure they are well spaced out. Brush them over with a smear of beaten egg and bake in a hot oven (450°F/Gas 8) for about 10 minutes.

THE GREEN TEA ROOM

The Green Tea Room is a truly gracious room. It overlooks the most beautiful sweep of lawn, flowerbeds and trees in the palace gardens. Situated at the far north-west corner of the palace, it is a lofty room, full of light and colour. The fact that it is called a 'tea room' is a misnomer, as the Queen and Prince Philip use it for nearly all their family meals, as well as for entertaining close friends and relatives. Until 1956, when it was redecorated, it was known as the Queen's Chippendale Room and much of the furnishings remain predominantly Chippendale. It also features magnificent carvings and embellishments on the ceiling and walls, which are covered with soft-coloured tapestries.

Lemon Curd Sponge

lemon curd
4 eggs
4 oz sugar
3 ½ oz plain flour
1 oz melted butter

Break the eggs into a large basin, then place the basin in a pan of hot water. Whisk the contents and add the sugar briskly until light and fluffy but sufficiently stiff to retain the impression of a whisk for a few seconds. Remove the basin from the heat and sieve in one-third of the flour, gently folding it into the mixture using a metal spoon. The remaining flour should be folded in with equal care. Finally add the melted butter, which must be runny but not too hot. Pour the mixture into a greased 7-inch cake tin, place in a moderate oven (350°F/Gas 4) and bake for about 1 hour. Wait until the cake is cold, then cut it in half and fill it with lemon curd before sandwiching the two halves together.

Currant Buns

1 ¾ lb flour
4 oz currants
1 oz chopped peel
1 beaten egg
4 oz castor sugar
¾ pint milk and water,
    lukewarm
1 oz yeast
4 oz margarine
milk and sugar to glaze
1 teaspoon salt

Sieve ½ lb of the flour into a bowl. Cream 1 teaspoon of sugar with yeast and stir in the lukewarm liquid. Strain into the flour and mix thoroughly. Cover and put in a warm place to set for 45 minutes. When it has risen well, stir in the rest of the flour, then mix in fat, egg, fruit, salt and sugar. Thoroughly beat the mixture by hand, then cover and leave it to rise for about 1 hour. When it has almost doubled in size, flour your hands and shape small portions of dough into buns. Place the buns on a greased baking sheet and allow them to stand in a warm place for 30 minutes. Then bake in a hot oven (450°F/Gas 8). When almost cooked, brush with milk and sugar to glaze.

Sablés à la Poche

5 ½ oz plain flour
2 ½ oz icing sugar
1 egg yolk
3 ½ oz butter
1 oz ground almonds
pinch vanilla sugar
1 tablespoon milk (approx)
pinch baking powder

Sieve the icing sugar and flour together. In the centre of the heap make a well and in it put the egg yolk, butter, ground almonds, vanilla sugar and baking powder. Carefully add milk and work with the fingers until a soft paste has been made. Beat well and transfer to a forcing bag fitted with a large rosette pipe. Pipe out the mixture into rounds on a lightly greased baking sheet, and bake in a moderate oven (350°F/Gas 4) for about 15 minutes, or until set firm. Set out on a wire rack and remove to a cool place.

Alternatively this mixture can be put in a refrigerator to harden for about 2 hours and then rolled out and cut with a 2-inch fancy cutter. The shapes are then baked as plain biscuits.

Pont Neuf

For the crème patisserie:
6 egg yolks
7 oz sugar
1 vanilla pod
1 pint milk
2 ½ oz sifted flour

Fill tartlet cases with shortcrust pastry, then prick it with a fork. Into each case put a mixture of equal quantities of pâté à chou and crème patisserie, stirred together while very cold. Make sure the filling is arranged so that its surface is not level with the top of the case, but gently mounded in the centre. Roll out and trim a thin ribbon of short pastry and lay two little strips crossways over each filled pont neuf. Bake in a moderate oven for about 15 minutes.

TO MAKE CRÈME PATISSERIE:

Heat but don't boil the milk and add the vanilla pod. Allow it to soak in the milk until it has acquired a marked vanilla flavour. Whisk the egg yolks and sugar together in a saucepan and when blended add the flour. Gradually beat the ingredients steadily until all are combined. Bring the milk to the boil, remove the vanilla pod, then slowly beat it in to the yolk-flour-sugar mixture. Place the saucepan over a moderate heat and continue whisking until it is of a firm, creamy texture. Allow it to cool, stirring occasionally.

Eclairs au Café

3 oz flour (plain or self-raising)
2 whole eggs and yolk of 1 egg
    or 3 small eggs
1 oz butter
¼ pint water
pinch sugar

For the icing:
1 dessertspoon strong
    warm coffee
6 oz icing sugar

First, make the choux pastry. Gently heat the butter, sugar and water in a saucepan until the butter has completely melted. Remove from the heat and stir in the flour. Now return the pan to a low heat and cook very gently, stirring ceaselessly until the mixture is thoroughly cooked and dry enough to form a ball, and leave the pan clean.

Once again remove the mixture from the heat and gradually add the well-beaten eggs, stirring steadily to ensure a perfectly smooth mixture. Stand until well

cooled then pipe the mixture into finger shapes on well-greased and floured baking trays. (Or put into greased and floured finger tins if available.) Bake, uncovered, for 25 minutes. When cooked, split, fill with cream and coat with coffee icing.

TO MAKE THE ICING:

Slowly add the warm coffee to the icing sugar (sieve if lumpy), mixing until the correct consistency is reached – the icing should be thick enough to coat the back of a spoon.

Small Chocolate Cakes

5 oz flour
1 oz cocoa
chocolate shavings
3 oz margarine
3 oz sugar
1 egg
1 teaspoon baking powder
white glacé icing
milk to mix

Cream the fat and sugar together, then thoroughly beat in the egg. Sieve the dry ingredients and add them, along with the milk, to give a soft, dropping consistency. Transfer the mixture to paper baking cases and bake in a moderate oven (350°F/Gas 4) for 20-25 minutes. Allow the cakes to become quite cold before adding a little icing to each one. When this has almost set, sprinkle with chocolate shavings.

TO MAKE THE ICING:

In a small pan, stir 4 oz of sieved icing sugar into 1 tablespoon of water over heat until warm but not hot. When it turns glossy and coats the back of a wooden spoon evenly, it is ready to use.

THE TALE OF MAGGIE SMITH

The tea services and silverware used by the Queen and her guests are the responsibility of the china pantry and silver pantry, but for many years they were jealously guarded by an elderly spinster known as Maggie Smith (real name Norah), proud of her official title of Coffee Room Maid. She kept all the tea things locked away in a big white wooden cabinet, which no footman or page, not even Prince Philip, dared go near. For at least three generations Maggie Smith — short, plump, rosy-cheeked and with thick-lensed glasses — kept an eagle eye on proceedings at royal teas, ensuring without fail that her tea things returned to roost. For many years she had the unofficial title of Queen's Tea Maker, though in fact she did no such thing.

But for all her great pride in her daily duty, Maggie Smith's finest hour was undoubtedly Christmas time at Sandringham, where she became the official toast maker for the royal caviar! Although the royal family are not regular eaters of caviar, they always have it during the Christmas holiday period, when they receive gifts of Portuguese caviar. Maggie Smith would ensure that the toast was just right — done to a turn, with an even golden brown all over, and served piping hot. This was often a tense moment for 'Maggie' and beforehand she could be seen pacing the kitchen floor, clasping and unclasping her hands in anxiety. During the half-hour that she performed her task she would insist that an under-butler remain close beside her, ready to perform his part in quickly transporting the freshly made toast.

During her normal duties at the palace, only two cups and saucers regularly escaped the vigilance of Maggie Smith for as long as nine hours at a time. These were the ones served to the Queen and Prince Philip for their customary nightcap, a pot of tea, which is placed by the side of their bed along with a kettle. It is usual for the Prince to boil the water and make the tea, before the two of them sit and chat before settling down for the night. Unfortunately for Maggie, she could not reclaim her precious china until 9 a.m. the following day.

Scotch Bread

1 lb flour

1 lb sugar

1 lb butter

8 eggs

½ lb candied lemon, orange
and citron peel in equal
proportions

gill Cognac brandy

pinch salt

4 oz white comfits

Using a wooden spoon, work the butter in a basin until it has the appearance of thick cream. Gradually add the flour, sugar, eggs and salt. When the whole is thoroughly mixed, add the candied peel (cut in shreds), the brandy and the rind of two oranges or lemons (rubbed on sugar). Pour the paste into oblong-shaped tins, about 2 inches deep and coated with butter. After the comfits have been scattered over the surface, shake a little fine sugar over the top just before placing the tins on baking sheets in the oven. Bake until the mixture turns a very light brown.

Note: This kind of cake is a general favourite in Scotland, being served on most occasions, at breakfast, luncheon, dinner, or as a casual refreshment.

Sandringham Christmas Cake

1 Ib sultanas
1 Ib currants
10 eggs
1 Ib butter
12 oz sugar
1 Ib cut and stoned raisins
½ Ib cut peel
1 Ib glacé cherries
1 Ib ground almonds
1 Ib flour
1 oz mixed spices
nutmeg
1 teaspoonful salt
glass brandy

Cream the butter and add to it the other ingredients. Stir thoroughly and bake in a moderate oven for about 2 ½ hours. When cold, cover with almond paste, made by mixing 1 ½ lb of ground almond with 1 ½ lb of icing sugar and 6 egg whites. Then cover all over with royal icing, which is made by vigorously beating 6 oz of icing sugar with 3 egg whites. Leave the cake to set for a day or two in a cool, dry place.

Albert Biscuits

10 oz pounded sugar
8 oz lightly chopped almonds
6 oz flour
12 egg yolks
14 egg whites
2 oz candied orange peel,
    finely shred
1 teaspoon cinnamon powder
½ teaspoon ground cloves
grated lemon rind

Work the sugar and almonds with the egg yolks and 2 egg whites for 20 minutes. Then incorporate the remaining 12 whites, firmly whisked together with the flour, candied peel and spices. Next, pour the batter into a convenient-sized paper case, and bake it in a moderate oven. When done and sufficiently cold, cut it into thin slices for dishing up. This preparation may also be baked in small moulds, or forced out on to paper or baking sheets previously buttered and floured for the purpose.

Victoria Biscuits

1 lb pounded sugar
12 oz dried flour
6 oz pounded or ground
    bitter almonds
6 oz fresh butter
wine glass kirschwasser
rind 2 lemons

First, with a wooden spoon work up the butter up in a basin, until it assumes a creamy appearance, then add the remainder of the ingredients, finishing with the kirschwasser. When the batter is ready, pour it into small moulds that have been coated with butter and potato flour, and bake it in a moderate oven until the cakes, or biscuits, turn a very light colour. First, spread the surface with orange marmalade, then glaze them according to the directions given for finishing Apricot Biscuits.

Soup

Potage Parmentier

2 leeks
3 cups potatoes, cut in quarters
1 quart white stock
3 tablespoons cream or stock
6 tablespoons butter
1 tablespoon chervil leaves

Take the white parts of the leeks only and shred them. Melt 2 tablespoons of butter in a saucepan and lightly cook the leeks. Now add the potatoes and moisten with stock. Season to taste and boil rapidly until the potatoes are cooked. Mash the potatoes and rub through a sieve. Add 2 or 3 tablespoons of cream or stock, and finish off with the remainder of the butter and the chervil leaves. Serve with croûtons crisply fried in butter.

Cream of Pea Soup

2 cups split peas

1 teaspoon salt

1 tablespoon butter

½ cup salt pork, finely diced

1 medium onion, finely
chopped

1 medium carrot, finely
chopped

2 leeks (green tops), finely
chopped

1 cup spinach, finely chopped

1 bay leaf

pinch thyme

1 cup stock

1 teaspoon sugar

1 tablespoon butter

½ cup double cream

Allow the split peas to soak in water for just over an hour. Drain off the water and put the peas into a large saucepan with 1 quart of fresh water and a teaspoon of salt. Bring to the boil and skim the water, then cover and simmer steadily. Melt the butter in a soup kettle and add the salt pork. Cook until the pork begins to brown. Add the onion and sauté until soft but not brown, then add the chopped vegetables. Pop in a bay leaf and a pinch of thyme.

Cook for a few minutes, then pour in the partly cooked peas with their water. Continue to cook for about 1 hour, or until the peas are very soft. Pour the soup through a fine sieve and add the stock, then bring back to the boil. Season to taste with salt and add the sugar, butter and double cream.

If fresh peas are available, cook 1 cup in water until soft and rub them through a sieve into the soup. If they are very young and small, include the pods.

Soupe à l'Oignon

(Serves 4-6 people)

3 large onions
2 oz butter
2 oz cheese, grated
1 heaped teaspoon plain flour
1 teaspoon castor sugar
2–2 ½ pints water
French bread slices
seasoning

Slice the onions into thin rings. In a thick pan, heat the butter then add the onion rings and season well. Keep stirring carefully over a medium heat, taking care not to burn the onions, until their colour changes to golden brown. This should take at least 20 minutes. Next steadily add the flour, stirring all the time. Pour in the water and sugar, and allow the pan to simmer gently for 15 minutes.

Spread the slices of French bread with a thin layer of butter then evenly cover them with grated cheese. Now arrange them in a hot soup tureen and carefully pour in the soup. Cover the tureen and keep it warm for 5 minutes before serving.

VARIATIONS:

Sieve the onions before pouring the soup into the tureen.

Evenly brown the bread and cheese beneath a hot grill before placing in the tureen.

Use vegetable stock instead of water and good dripping instead of butter.

Consommé aux Quenelles

A quenelle is a small seasoned ball of fish or meat forcemeat, which is made by pounding the ingredients in a mortar, then binding it with eggs. To make 2 quarts of the consommé you will need:

chicken carcass and giblets
½ cup leeks (white part), diced
1 ½ lb lean beef (with gristle and fat removed), chopped
1 egg white
1 large carrot, diced
3 quarts plus 1 cup stock

Put the diced vegetables into a saucepan with the chopped meat and the egg white. Mix well before pouring in the stock. Bring to the boil, stirring constantly with a wooden spoon, then draw the saucepan to the edge of the heat and simmer very slowly for 1 ½ hours. Skin off any surplus fat and strain through muslin. Sprinkle with chopped chervil leaves before serving.

Crème de Céleri

1 lb crisp white celery
1 ¼ pints béchamel
1 oz butter
1 ½ pints white stock
cream

Mince the celery (discarding any green or discoloured pieces) and reserve 2 tablespoons for garnish. Parboil them, drain, then stew in the butter. Mix in the béchamel and complete the cooking slowly. Strain through a sieve and add the white stock. Now heat almost to a boil and finish by adding cream just before serving. Garnish with diced celery.

Consommé Tomate Froid

1 ½ lb tomatoes
½ small beetroot, preferably
    uncooked
small piece of celery
1 small onion, chopped
1 pint water or white stock
1 teaspoon vinegar or
    lemon juice
Worcestershire sauce
    (few drops)
bay leaves
seasoning

Put all the ingredients together in a large saucepan and simmer carefully for about 25 minutes, by which time the tomatoes should be very soft. Now remove the beetroot and bay leaves and rub the rest through a sieve. Complete by straining through muslin. If a slightly thicker soup is preferred, omit the final straining stage. Thoroughly chill before serving.

Consommé Cyrano

First prepare 1 quart of consommé with a fumet of duck. Carefully shape 12 small quenelles of duck forcemeat so that they are uniformly flat and oval. Poach the quenelles, drain, then transfer to a small, shallow earthen dish. Sprinkle with a little grated Parmesan cheese and a few drops of chicken glaze. Put them in the oven until well glazed.

The quenelles should be served separately in the dish in which they were glazed.

FOOD FOR THE CHILDREN

When Prince Charles and Princess Anne were younger, suppertime would be at 7 p.m. sharp, wherever they happened to be. This meant they had to be washed and in their nightclothes, ready for bed, immediately after supper.

Favourite nursery suppers – apart from leek soup and potatoes followed by fruit and custard – were clear soup and toast, or sago pudding and pears. In such a setting, even sausages and baked beans acquired the distinguished status of a royal dish! Barley water has always been a favourite drink of the royal household, particularly by the Queen and her children when younger, and it is not by coincidence that the English manufacturer Robinsons has continued to supply the household for many, many years.

From an early age, Prince Charles developed an unusual interest in cooking and what went on in the kitchen. When he was ten, he regularly visited the chefs. Weighing ingredients, and fetching dishes, pots and pans were chores in which he delighted from infancy. He would also give warning when kettles, pots and saucepans were coming to the boil. Princess Anne, with far less interest in kitchen activities, made sporadic appearances, and would aid her brother, bringing from the store cupboards various items the chefs had listed on a piece of paper.

Away from the royal household, while at boarding school, Princess Anne acquired a taste for fish and chips, and especially fish and chips served in the traditional manner – wrapped in newspaper!

Scotch Broth

Take a neck of fresh mutton and trim it as you would for cutlets. Transfer the scrag and trimmings to a pan, together with 2 carrots, 3 turnips, 2 heads of celery, 2 onions, a bunch of parsley and a sprig of thyme, and cook into a broth – topping up with either water or broth from the common stockpot.

While the broth is boiling, cut up the neck of mutton into chops, removing surplus skin and fat, and place in a 3-quart stew pan. Next cut into very small dice the red or outer part of 2 carrots, 3 turnips, 2 leeks, 1 onion and 2 heads of celery, and add to the pan. Also add 6 oz of Scotch barley, previously washed and parboiled. Then strain and remove fat from the broth before pouring it into the stew pan.

Allow the soup to boil gently until the chops and the vegetables are thoroughly cooked. Five minutes before serving the soup, throw in a tablespoon of chopped and blanched parsley. Be sparing in your use of salt, so as not to overpower the simple but sweet flavour that characterizes this delicious broth.

Nutritious Liquid Custard of Chicken

Prepare the chicken broth as directed for making chicken custards, and thoroughly mix ½ a pint with 2 yolks of freshly laid eggs. Stir it over the stove-fire, or, if practicable, over the heat of steam, until the mixture becomes somewhat thickened, assuming a soft, creamy appearance. Pour it into a broth basin and serve immediately.

Cream of Pearl Barley à la Victoria

Wash 1 lb of pearl barley several times, blanch and drain on a sieve. Allow cold water to run over it for a few minutes, then put it into a stew pan with 2 quarts of white consommé of fowls. Set it to boil by the side of a slow fire for 4 hours. When the barley is sufficiently done so that it may be easily bruised, set a third of it aside in a small soup pot, and immediately rub the remainder through a tammy. Then mix the cream of barley with the whole barley that has been set aside. Ten minutes before serving the soup, add ½ pint of boiling cream.

Cream of Rice à la Cardinal

Prepare the cream of rice in the usual way, then mix in a good tablespoonful of crayfish or lobster butter and the juice of half a lemon. Pour into a soup tureen containing 30 tails of crayfish and 3 dozen very small quenelles of fowls.

Potato Soup à la Victoria

Prepare a purée of potatoes. When the dish is about ready send to the table, place three dozen small quenelles of potatoes in the soup tureen, with ½ pint of large heads of asparagus boiled green. Add the same proportion of French beans, cut into diamond shapes and boiled, then pour in the boiling purée and serve.

Cream of Rice à la Royale

Wash and blanch 1 lb of Carolina rice, drain, then put it in a stew pan with about 3 quarts of white consommé of fowls. Set it to boil on the stove and skim well, then place it to the side of the fire, allowing it to boil gently until the grains of rice are thoroughly done. Then rub the whole through a tammy, moistening with more broth if necessary, to form a purée. Transfer the purée into a small soup pot to clarify by ebullition, as if preparing a sauce. Just before sending it to the table, add ½ pint of boiling cream, and pour the soup into a tureen containing 1 dozen small custards of chicken.

To make the custards of chicken:

Roast a young fowl, then remove the whole of the breast and the white parts of the legs. Chop and pound them with a large spoonful of white sauce, then pass this through a tammy using a wooden spoon to form a purée. Next transfer the purée to a quart basin, together with 8 egg yolks, a little grated nutmeg and salt. Stir together well, mix with ½ pint of consommé of fowls, then pour the preparation into 12 small dariole moulds (previously buttered). Set the moulds carefully in a fricandeau pan, containing sufficient boiling water to half-cover the moulds. Put the lid on the pan, and place it either on a very moderate fire (in which case, live embers of charcoal must be put on the lid) or in the oven. About 10 minutes will suffice to poach the custards, when they must be turned out of the moulds on to a napkin. Afterwards place them in a soup tureen, then pour the purée over them.

Cream of Rice à la Victoria

Prepare the cream of rice as directed in Cream of Rice à la Royale. Twenty minutes before serving add about ¼ lb of whole rice (well boiled in white consommé of fowls) and boil it in the purée for 20 minutes. Just before serving, mix in 1 pint of boiling cream and a pat of fresh butter.

Hare Soup à la St George

Fillet 2 good-sized leverets and place the fillets in a small sauté pan with a little fresh butter, salt and pepper. Cover them with a round of buttered paper, and put them in the larder until dinnertime. Reserve a sufficient quantity of meat from the leveret's hindquarters to make some quenelles. Cut the remainder into small pieces and lightly fry them. Add an ample amount of flour to thicken the sauce of the soup, then moisten with a bottle of claret and 2 quarts of blond of veal. Add a garnished bouquet made with basil, marjoram, parsley, bay leaf, thyme, four cloves, mace and four shallots.

Let the sauce boil, skim well and, when the hare is thoroughly done, pass the sauce through a tammy into a soup pot. Place the pot on the fire to throw off any remaining roughness and allow it to reduce if necessary. Then pour it into a soup tureen containing 3 dozen small quenelles (made from the meat reserved from the leveret's hindquarters) and the scallops of hare prepared by lightly frying the fillets in the sauté pan. Taste to check the seasoning and serve.

PALACE LUNCHES

Palace lunches were introduced by the present Queen and are informal lunches without pomp or ceremony, with a wide variety of guests. There are usually around eight guests who, after chatting with the Queen over drinks for a short time, sit down with the royal couple at an oval table. The lunch consists of four courses, and a typical menu offers smoked salmon, roast veal with peas and carrots, apple meringue, and cheese and biscuits. Coffee, with port and brandy for those who want them, is served afterwards in the Bow Room. 'I had thought it would be a toffee-nosed affair, but it turned out to be a happy family lunch,' was the comment of a millionaire business tycoon. 'The Queen made me feel absolutely at home. She took me to the window to look at the gardens and laughed a great deal when I said it would be a fine site for development.'

The Queen gives eight or nine of her lunches every year, and has done so since 1957. Usually they are held in the lovely white and gold 1844 Room, looking out on the lawns and trees at the rear of the palace.

51

Calf's Feet Soup à la Windsor

Place in a 2-gallon stockpot a knuckle of lean ham, 2 calf's feet and 1 old hen (whose fillets will be used for making quenelles). Add 2 carrots, 2 onions stuck with 4 cloves, celery, and a bouquet of parsley, green onions, sweet basil and lemon thyme tied neatly together. Moisten with ½ bottle of light French white wine and place the stockpot on a moderate fire to boil for about 10 minutes. Top it up from the common stock or any white broth you may have ready, set it to boil on the stove and skim it well.

After 4 hours of gentle ebullition, remove the calf's feet and put them in water to clean them. Take out all the bones and lay them on a dish to cool before trimming, leaving the inner part of the feet only. All the outer skin should be thinly pared off so that the feet have a more transparent appearance. Cut them into pieces 1 inch length by ½ inch width, and set them to one side in a small soup pot until required.

Strain the consommé through a napkin, thicken it moderately with a little white roux, then add a little essence of mushrooms. Finish by incorporating a liaison of 6 egg yolks mixed with a little grated Parmesan and ½ pint of cream. Squeeze in the juice of ½ a lemon, and season with a little crystallized soluble cayenne. Pour the soup into a tureen containing 2 dozen very small quenelles (made from the hen fillets), some boiled macaroni cut into inch lengths, and the tendons of the calf's feet, previously warmed in a little consommé with ½ glass of white wine. Stir the soup gently in the tureen to mix the ingredients together, and serve.

Turtle Soup

Procure a fine, lively fat turtle weighing about 120 lb – fish of this weight being considered the best, as their fat is not liable to be impregnated with that disagreeable strong savour objected to in fish of larger size. On the other hand, very small turtle seldom possess sufficient fat or substance to make them worth dressing.

When time permits, kill the turtle overnight so that it may be left to bleed in a cool place until the next morning, when at an early hour it should be cut up for scalding – the first part of the operation. If, however, the turtle is required for immediate use, to save time the fish may be scalded as it is killed.

The turtle being ready for cutting up, lay it on its back and with a large kitchen knife separate the fat or belly-shell from the back by making an incision all around the inner edge of the shell. When all the fleshy parts adhering to the shell have been carefully cut away, it may be set aside.

Then detach the intestines by running the sharp edge of a knife closely along the spine of the fish, and remove them instantly in a pail, to be thrown away. Cut off the fins and separate the fleshy parts, which should be placed on a dish until required. Take particular care of every particle of the green fat, which lies chiefly at the sockets of the fore-fins, and more or less all around the interior of the fish, if in good condition. Let this fat, which, when in a healthy state, is elastic and of a bluish colour while raw, be steeped for several hours in cold water so that it may be thoroughly cleansed from all impurities.

Then with a meat saw divide the upper and under shells into manageable pieces, put them together with the fins and head into a large vessel containing boiling water, and quickly scald them. By this means they will be separated from the horny substance that covers them, which can then be easily removed. Then put them into a larger stockpot nearly filled with fresh hot water, and leave to continue boiling by the side of the stove-fire until the glutinous substance separates easily from the bones. Place the pieces of turtle carefully upon clean dishes and put them in the larder to cool. Then cut into sections about 1 ½ inch square – these will be added to the soup when it is nearly finished. Return the bones to the broth to boil for an hour longer, for the double purpose of extracting their entire savour and to effect the reduction of the turtle stock, which is to be used for filling up the turtle stockpot.

In order to save time, while the above is in operation, the turtle stock or consommé should be prepared as follows:

Melt 2 ½ oz of fresh butter in a stockpot, then add ¼ lb of raw ham cut in slices, 2 lb of leg of beef, a small knuckle of veal, and 1 old hen (after removing the fillets, which are to be kept for making quenelles). Then add all the fleshy pieces of the turtle (except those pieces intended for entrées), and place the head and fins on top. Moisten the whole with a glass of Madeira and 3 quarts of good stock. Add a handful of mushrooms, 3 or 4 cloves, a blade of mace, and a good-sized bouquet of parsley tied up with two bay leaves, a sprig of thyme, green onions and shallots. Set the consommé on a brisk fire to boil sharply and, when the liquid has reduced to a glaze, fill the stockpot up instantly with enough liquor to cover. As soon as it boils, skim it thoroughly, garnish with the usual proportion of vegetables, and remove it to the side of the stove to boil gently for 6 hours. Remember to probe the head and fins after they have been boiling for 2 hours. As soon as they are done, drain them on a dish, cover with a wet napkin well saturated with water to prevent it from sticking to them, and store them away in a cool place with the remainder of the glutinous parts of the turtle.

The stockpot should now be filled up with the reserved turtle broth. When the turtle stock is done, strain it off into an appropriate-sized stockpot, remove every particle of fat from the surface, then thicken it with a proportionate quantity of white roux to the consistency of thin sauce. Make this in exactly the same manner as directed for espagnole or brown

sauce in order to extract all the butter and scum, and give it a brilliant appearance.

Two glasses of old Madeira must now be added, together with a purée of herbs as follows:

Sweet basil must form one-third of the bunch of herbs, with equal quantities of winter savoury, marjoram and lemon-thyme making up the remaining two-thirds. To these add 1 tablespoonful of parsley, 2–3 green onions, 4–6 green shallots and some trimmings of mushrooms. Moisten with 1 pint of broth, and after stewing the herbs for about 1 hour, rub the whole through a tammy or fine sieve to form a purée. Add the purée to the soup and season with a pinch of cayenne pepper. Allow the pieces of turtle as well as the fins (also cut into small pieces with the larger bones removed) to boil in the soup for ¼ hour, then carefully remove the scum as it rises to the surface. Season according to taste.

To excel in dressing turtle, it is necessary to be very accurate in the proportions of the numerous ingredients used for seasoning this soup. Nothing should predominate, but the whole should be harmoniously blended.

Put the turtle away in basins, dividing the fat (after it has been scalded and boiled in some of the sauce) in equal quantities into each basin. Also add some small quenelles, which are to be made using the fillets of hen and, in addition to the usual ingredients, 2 yolks of hard-boiled eggs. Mould the quenelles into small, round balls to imitate turtles' eggs. Roll them by hand on a marble slab or table using a little flour, and poach them in the usual way.

When the turtle soup is wanted for use, warm it, and just before serving add a small glass of sherry or Madeira, and the juice of 1 lemon to every 4 quarts of turtle.

PURÉES OF POULTRY & GAME

Purée of Fowl à la Reine

Roast 2 good-sized young fowls, and take the meat off the bones. Chop and pound it thoroughly with ½ lb of boiled rice, then dilute it with 3 pints of chicken broth, made from the skins and carcasses of the 2 fowls. Using 2 wooden spoons, rub it through a tammy into a large dish. Transfer the purée into a soup pot, and store it in the larder until dinnertime. When required, warm it – being careful to prevent its curdling – then mix with it a pint of boiling cream, taste to check the seasoning, and serve.

Purée of Fowl à la Princess

Prepare the purée of fowl in the usual manner, mix in the boiling cream, then pour into a tureen containing 3 dozen very small quenelles of fowl and 4 oz of Frankfurt pearl barley, which has been well blanched and boiled for 2 hours in white chicken broth. Check that the seasoning is delicate, and send to the table.

Purée of Pheasants à la Royale

Roast a brace of pheasants, then remove the fillets and white part of the legs, and make a consommé with the remainder. Pound the meat with a proportionate quantity of boiled rice, dilute with the consommé, then rub the purée through a tammy. Finish with a small amount of game glaze, or essence, and serve accompanied by the usual plate of croûtons.

AN ITALIAN SOUP

Macaroni Soup à la Royale

Boil 10 oz of Naples macaroni in 2 quarts of boiling water, with 2 oz of fresh butter, salt and a little mignonette pepper. When the macaroni has boiled for ½ hour, drain it through a sieve, cut it into ½-inch lengths, then boil it in 2 quarts of good chicken or game consommé for 10 minutes. Take it off the stove and mix with it a leason of 6 egg yolks, ½ pint of cream, 2 oz of grated Parmesan cheese, and a pinch of mignonette pepper. Set the leason in the soup by stirring it on the stove-fire for 3 minutes, then serve.

Vermicelli or any other Italian pasta may be substituted for the macaroni. This dish is sometimes referred to as 'Soup à l'Italienne'.

COMMENTS FOR THE KITCHEN

When clearing away after a royal meal the footmen always look for the notebook in which the Queen or Prince Philip jot down comments for the kitchen. The book is always left on a small round wooden table. Once, on a torn-off top sheet, the footmen found the dead body of a slug. 'I found this in the salad – could you eat it?' the Queen had written on the pad! Mostly, the book remains blank, as the Queen is not fussy about food. However, when she has a guest to an informal lunch and they reveal definite likes and dislikes – such as an objection to fried potatoes or Brussels sprouts – the Queen will make a discreet note for future reference. This is duly recorded by the kitchen and remembered, should the guest come again. If Prince Philip especially likes a wine, or his wife is particularly complimentary, he will write on the bottle label 'Good' or 'Very Good' so that the Yeoman of the Wine Cellars will know to serve it again.

PANADAS AND LIGHT SOUPS FOR INFANTS AND INVALIDS

Chicken Panada

Roast a young fowl, remove all the white meat, then pound it with French bread crumbs soaked in broth. Dilute with a little chicken broth (made from the remains of the roasted fowl) to the consistency of a soft batter or creamy substance, then pass it through a tammy, as if preparing any other purée. Prior to serving, panada should be moderately warmed and put into custard cups. When preparing any kind of dietetic preparation for infants and invalids, it is necessary to avoid the use of herbs, vegetables and spices – even salt should be used sparingly.

Pheasant or Partridge Panada

Prepare in the same manner as described for making Chicken Panada, substituting game for poultry.

Ceylon Moss Gelatinous Chicken Broth

Cut a fowl into four parts, take out the lungs, and wash thoroughly. Place it in a stewpan with 4 oz of prepared Ceylon moss, adding 3 pints of water and a little salt. Boil the broth for ¾ hour by the side of a stove-fire, pass it through a napkin, and serve it in a caudle cup.

Nutritious Liquid Custard of Game

Prepare in the same way as described for Liquid Custard of Chicken, substituting pheasant or partridge for poultry.

Chicken or Game Custards

Cut a young fowl into quarters, remove the lungs, and wash thoroughly. Place it in a stewpan with a little parsley, chervil, ½ head of celery and 1 turnip. Fill the stewpan with 3 pints of cold water, place it on the fire and, as soon as it boils, skim it thoroughly. Set the pan by the side of the fire to remain boiling for an hour, then strain the broth into a basin through a napkin, and use it in the following manner:

According to the number of custard cups required, place so many egg yolks in a basin. Add the same number of custard-cupfuls of prepared chicken broth and beat these together with a spoon or fork. Next, use pressure to pass them through a tammy. Fill the custard cups, steam them in the usual manner, and quickly serve. The custards should be eaten soon after being made, as they become heavy when warmed a second time.

Venison Panada

Take approximately 1 lb of the lean part of either a roasted haunch or neck of venison. Mince it, then pound it with French-bread crumbs soaked in good broth. Dilute with a little consommé and pass the panada through a tammy. Just before serving the panada, warm carefully to prevent it from becoming somewhat decomposed and rough, and rather indigestible for a delicate stomach.

Savouries

DINNER FOR ONE

When the Prince is away and the Queen dines alone at Buckingham Palace, she often prefers to have just a light snack. Although the menu book will offer three courses – fish, meat, and sweet or savoury – the Queen will order just the fish or the meat course and nothing more. Often she will settle for just a savoury – perhaps flaked smoked haddock in scrambled egg, served with a thin piece of toast.

WHEN THE PRINCE DOES THE COOKING

The royal kitchens have always experimented with new dishes and, during the present Queen's reign, this has largely been at the instigation of Prince Philip, who usually returns with alternative recipe suggestions after trips abroad on a state tour or visit.

Yorkshire-born Ronald Aubrey, who for many years served as the royal chef, knew that if a new dish didn't arrive at the royal table exactly as the Prince remembered it, there would be a visit to the kitchens and a searching discussion on exactly what went wrong. It was Prince Philip who insisted that Mr Aubrey go on a course at the Ritz Hotel, Paris, to learn some of the more advanced arts of the French chefs de cuisine. He later returned to the palace as a member of the Confrérie de la Chaine des Rôtisseurs (Brotherhood of Turning Spit Masters).

Sometimes the Prince experiments with preparing and cooking dishes he has particularly enjoyed on his travels, but he is also fond of what he terms good, simple cooking – such as a casserole of pigeons, cooked according to a Swedish recipe. His most ambitious dish was a snipe, which, after shooting it at Sandringham, he plucked, cleaned and prepared himself.

Breakfast and supper snacks are his specialities. Wherever he goes, he insists on his electric glass-covered frying pan being packed so that he can do the cooking. For breakfast, bacon, eggs and sausages are his usual raw materials, though he often cooks kidneys and omelettes. The Prince is also adept at producing quick, light supper snacks, which he and the Queen often enjoy after they have dismissed the servants for the night. Dishes include scrambled eggs and smoked haddock, mushrooms sautéed in butter with bacon, Scotch woodcock with mushrooms, and omelette with bacon.

However, Prince Philip's first love is open-air barbecue cooking – usually just for picnics, but sometimes full-scale camping jaunts. When the children were younger he would take them off to the lonely moors above Balmoral, the Land Rover packed with sleeping bags, basic provisions such as milk, tea, sugar, bread, sausages, eggs and bacon, and his mobile barbecue equipment. They would camp in a little stone shelter hut specially built for royal picnics in the days of Queen Victoria. Water for tea and washing was fetched by the children from a nearby burn, and boiled over a fire of dried heather and twigs. High in the hills above Balmoral there is a dark and mysterious loch called Loch Muick, which has been a frequent picnic spot for the Queen and Prince Philip since the first time they went to Balmoral together. Travelling on hill ponies they would make the trek to this haunting place of mountain streams, where the eerie calling of the red grouse can be heard.

Large picnic parties for the royal family and their friends were frequent events at Balmoral. The food was loaded on to Land Rovers, which were used to take the royal party out to the moors. Once his barbecue grill was glowing, Prince Philip would produce a rapid succession of sizzling chops, steaks and sausages for guests and attendant staff. If there was a nearby stream, the Queen would also insist on doing most of the washing up – much to the dismay of the staff.

Game Pie has always been a particular favourite on picnics and royal shooting parties at Windsor and Sandringham, as well as Balmoral. From late summer to mid winter Prince Philip spends as much time shooting as his busy schedule permits. During August and September it is principally grouse that is shot, but among other game at Balmoral are ptarmigan, and invariably capercaillie and woodcock in the dark forests around Balmoral Castle.

Woodcock Pie

The custom of presenting the monarch with a woodcock pie appears to have started with Lord Talbot, Viceroy of Ireland, in 1813. He presented four-and-twenty woodcocks baked in a pie to King George III. There is also on record the gift of woodcock pie sent to King George V during Christmas 1920 by Mr James McNeill, Governor General of the Irish Free State.

4 woodcock
½ lb fat bacon
¼ lb veal
2 thick sections raw carrot
salt, pepper and spice

First pluck the woodcocks, retaining 2 unplucked heads to set on top when the pie is ready for the table (or four if the pie is made with eight birds or more). Singe each bird then remove the trail (which should also be retained), gizzard and bone.

Although the pie crust can be made according to individual tastes, a recommended one for Woodcock Pie follows an old recipe for Melton Mowbray pies. The required ingredients are: a ratio of 3 ½ lb of flour to 1 lb of lard and 1 pint of water with 1 heaped teaspoon of salt. Boil the lard in the water and, as soon as the water boils, knead the lard, water and flour for ½ hour. Now place it in a pre-warmed earthen dish covered with a warm cloth for ½ hour.

It is essential that the pastry is kept warm, otherwise it crumbles and cannot be worked. Conversely, if it is too hot, it will be too soft to retain its shape once the pie crust has been moulded and decorated. For this reason great care must be taken when pouring the boiled water and lard into the flour to ensure that the pastry is both smooth and very stiff. Finally, it should be well beaten with a rolling pin. The prepared pie crust should be put into a mould, which can be opened at the side to remove the pie after baking.

Line the pie with the fat bacon, retaining 3 oz of this for the forcemeat and sufficient to cover the birds. The forcemeat is made with the bacon, veal and woodcock trail, pounded together in a mortar, and seasoned with salt, pepper and aromatic spices according to taste. Usually the spices would include cloves, nutmeg, mace, white peppercorns, bay leaves, thyme, basil and marjoram at a ratio of 2 oz of peppercorns and cloves to 1 oz each of the remaining spices, except the dried bay leaves, which should not exceed ½ oz.

Stuff the inside of each woodcock with the forcemeat, then lay the birds close together in the piecrust. Any noticeable gaps between the birds should be filled with forcemeat as well. Next carefully cover the woodcocks with the left over bacon, then place the decorated crust on top. Make a neat hole in the pie top, then put in a moderate oven and bake for 2 hours.

When the pie is cooked, pour in through the hole sufficient clear gravy, which will form a jelly when cold to fill the pie to the top. Allow to stand until cold and before serving decorate the top with 2 or more woodcock heads. These should be well cleaned and each neck replaced with a thick slice of raw carrot so that they will stand upright.

Spaghetti Bolognese

6–8 oz spaghetti
Parmesan cheese

For the Bolognese sauce:
1 can tomatoes
1 small can tomato purée
    approx. 6 oz minced beef
2 oz mushrooms, finely chopped
½ pint good brown stock
2 oz butter
1 onion, finely chopped
1 carrot, shredded
½–1 clove garlic (optional)
seasoning

Heat the butter in the pan, crush the garlic and gently fry it for 4-5 minutes along with the onion, mushrooms and carrot. Add the tomato purée and cook for a minute. Now stir in the minced beef and continue cooking until done. Add the stock and tomatoes, season to taste, and simmer until the sauce thickens.

The spaghetti should be cooked in briskly boiling salted water. Strain it and pour the sauce over it. Serve with grated Parmesan cheese.

Quiche Lorraine

6 oz flaky pastry
2 eggs
6 oz grated cheese
¼ pint cream
3 rashers bacon
¼ pint milk
seasoning

Cut the bacon into small pieces and fry them lightly. Line a deep flan ring with the pastry. Now beat the eggs and mix in the cream, milk, chopped bacon, grated cheese and seasoning. Pour this gently into the ring and place it in the centre of a medium-hot oven (375°F/Gas 5). When the filling has become firm and the pastry is well risen and a golden brown (after about 35 minutes), remove from oven. Quiche Lorraine is best served warm but not hot.

La Quiche Lorraine
(Traditional)

This is a recipe for the real Quiche Lorraine as made in country districts around the Vosges mountains.

First, make a short pastry using 7 oz of sieved flour, 2 oz of fresh butter, 1 ½ oz of lard (preferably pork), ½ gill of cold water, and a generous pinch of salt. Thoroughly mix the flour, butter and lard, with added salt, in a basin. Now carefully stir in the water. The resultant pastry should be an even and smooth paste. Roll out, mound together, then roll out again, trying to handle it as little as possible. Form the pastry into a mound a second time, and leave under a damp cloth in a cool larder for 1 hour. Then roll out the pastry again and arrange it in a deep metal flan dish some 12 inches in diameter.

Now take between 15 and 20 thin rashers of streaky bacon, remove the rind, and fry them gently in a little clarified butter in a covered frying pan for no more than a minute. Then completely line the pastry shell with the bacon. Pour 1 ½ gills of cream into a bowl and beat into it 2 large eggs and a pinch of salt. Pour this mixture into the flan dish and cook it in a hot oven for ½ hour, until it turns a rich golden brown. Allow the quiche to stand for about ½ hour before serving, to ensure that it is at exactly the right degree of warmth and that its fine full flavour is at its best.

Mushrooms Sautéd in Butter

Trim off the mushroom stalks level with the cap, then wash, dry and slice – do net peel. Season with salt and pepper.

Heat a knob of butter in a pan until hot but not brown. Cook the undersides of the mushroom caps first, which should take about 2 minutes. Then quickly turn to cook their rounded tops, which should take 3 minutes. Sprinkle with finely chopped parsley and serve.

Champignons à la Crème

1 lb mushrooms
butter
1 onion, chopped
cream

Cook the onion in butter, ensuring there is no discolouration. Add 2 dessert spoons of the onion to the mushrooms and stew together in butter. When they are cooked, drain and cover with boiling cream. Bring back to the boil and continue gently until the cream has been completely reduced. Just before removing, pour over a little warm thin cream, then serve.

Mushrooms à la Crème

(As per Prince Philip's recipe)

1 lb mushrooms
2 oz flour
2 oz butter
2 tablespoons cream
croutons
salt and pepper

Thoroughly clean and dry the mushrooms but don't peel. Slice them into a pan and simmer in butter for 5 minutes. Sprinkle with flour, stir gently and cook for a further 2 minutes or so. Season, add heated (but not boiled) milk and simmer for a further 3 minutes. Now stir in the cream, immediately reheat well, and serve scattered with croutons of fried bread.

Macaroni au Gratin

3 oz macaroni

2 oz cheese

1 oz butter

1 tablespoon crisp bread crumbs

seasoning

½ pint cheese sauce

For the cheese sauce:

1 oz butter

5 oz grated cheese

½ pint milk

salt and pepper

pinch mustard

Bring 1 ½ pints of water to a brisk boil, adding 1 level teaspoon of salt. Put in the macaroni and cook steadily, ensuring that it does not overcook — it should be just nicely tender. Now drain thoroughly and put in a hot serving dish.

While the macaroni is cooking the sauce should be made as follows:

Heat the butter gently until it is a clear, hot liquid, then remove from the heat and stir in the flour. Now cook carefully for a few minutes, ensuring that it does not brown. Remove from the heat again and gently blend in the cold milk. Next, bring to the boil and, stirring steadily with a wooden spoon, cook until it is smooth. Season liberally and, after the sauce has been allowed to thicken, thoroughly stir in the grated cheese and mustard.

The sauce should be poured over the drained macaroni the moment it has been put in the hot dish. Next sprinkle with the 2 oz of grated cheese and bread crumbs, and position nuts of butter evenly over the surface. Place the dish near the top of a fairly hot oven (400°F/Gas 6) and remove when it has crisply browned.

Sausage Rolls

6 oz flaky pastry
8 oz sausage meat
egg yolk or milk to glaze

Roll out the pasty into a long, even strip. Even out the sausage meat into a long roll and lay it down one side of the pastry. Fold the pastry over the meat and seal the edges. Slit the top at regular intervals and cut into individual rolls. Brush with milk or egg yolk and bake in a very hot oven (475°F/Gas 9) for 15 minutes or more, until nicely browned.

Ravioli au Parmesan

2 whole eggs
1 lb flour
2 tablespoons oil
1 egg yolk
sufficient water to make stiff
dough
pinch salt

For the filling:
small breast of chicken
veal
sweetbread
calf's brain
spinach
brown stock
1 tablespoon grated Parmesan
1 egg
garlic, chopped
1 bay leaf

Make a stiff dough with the flour, eggs and water, and knead for about 20 minutes. Allow to stand for 30 minutes, then roll it out very lightly on a floured board. Cut the pastry into rounds of about 3 inches in diameter and, on each, place a little stuffing made as follows:

Put the chicken breast, calf's brain and spinach into a saucepan along with the garlic, bay leaf, a little bread soaked in milk, and a small amount of stock, and braise. Allow to simmer gently for about 45 minutes until the stock is completely absorbed. Remove the by-now dry mixture from the saucepan and pound in a mortar, mixing with grated Parmesan cheese and finally binding with an egg.

Fold over the pastry and press the edges together, dampening a little to prevent the ravioli opening while cooking. Boil in stock for 20 minutes then remove and transfer to a hot dish. Pour over a sauce made with a little stock, thickened with meat glaze. Finally, sprinkle with Parmesan cheese.

PLATES AND SERVING DISHES

A special tray is used for occasions when the Queen is entertaining guests in the royal suite at Buckingham Palace. It is white with gold edging, and has a glass top under which are four colour photographs of the Queen's racehorses, named along with their jockeys: Doutelle with W.H. Carr; Aureole with E. Smith; Carozza with L. Piggott; and Pall Mall with D. Smith. Guests always admire the tray as a footman comes round with the drinks, and it proves to be a great conversation-prompter as discussion inevitably turns to racehorses, and the Queen's horses in particular – a favourite royal topic.

The magnificent gold and silver plate, meticulously maintained in the gold and silver pantries of Buckingham Palace, is used only on great occasions such as state banquets. But the Queen also likes gold plates to be used for serving sandwiches to guests when there is a film show at the palace, Windsor, Balmoral or Sandringham. Somehow eating sandwiches off gold plate seems to make them extra special.

Until the reign of King Edward VII, it was customary for the best solid silver, engraved with the royal crest, to be brought out even at the big garden parties held in the palace grounds. From time to time a few spoons would be unaccounted for, but these were casually written off as mislaid through the carelessness of servants. However, one day, after a large number of American guests had attended at the King's special invitation, literally hundreds of silver knives, forks and spoons bearing the royal insignia had vanished. The horrified silver pantry reported the loss of 1,000 teaspoons alone! Probing such a scandal could only be done discreetly, but the palace officials found that nearly all the articles had been taken by the Americans, among whom souvenir-hunting was all the rage at that time. King Edward coldly instructed that all his missing silver should be disreguarded, and that in future only ordinary plated cutlery without the royal crest should be put out for garden parties.

Formerly, on occasions such as the huge garden parties given by the Queen at the palace, it was necessary to retain large amounts of staff, with additional assistance provided by extra employees. For numerous reasons this proved impractical and incurred many problems as well as extra costs. In more recent times the catering for such large banquets has been supplemented by outside catering firms, and therefore the appropriate staff requirements for each event can be individually dealt with and planned. On such occasions only the royal family and immediate guests are provided for by the royal kitchens and the gold and silver pantries.

Anchovy Toasts

4–5 anchovies
3–4 slices toast
3 egg yolks
½ pint thin cream
salt and pepper

Cut the toast neatly into fingers and butter liberally. Keep them hot. Wash, scrape and bone the anchovies, then pound and chop them very finely. Spread evenly on the toast fingers. Beat the egg yolks with the cream, season with salt and pepper, then scramble in a double boiler until creamy. Arrange the toast on a hot dish and cover with the scrambled egg.

Marrow Toast

1 large marrow bone
chopped parsley
lemon juice
1 shallot, finely chopped
salt and pepper
sections of hot, crisp toast

This dish was a great favourite of Queen Victoria's, who required that it was prepared for dinner every day.

Break open the bone (or better still, get the butcher to do it) and extract marrow in lumps about the size of a cob nut. Parboil in slightly salted water for no longer than 1 minute. Drain quickly, if possible on a pre-warmed sieve, and keep warm. Season lightly with chopped parsley, lemon juice, a pinch of salt and pepper, and a soupçon of chopped shallot.

Gently toss the ingredients together, then spread on the hot toast and serve.

Ravioli au Jus

Boil the required amount of ravioli until it is three-quarters cooked, then drain. Pour over it a cup of brown veal or beef gravy and cover. Simmer slowly for about 15 minutes. Heap the ravioli on to a warmed serving dish and pour over it 2 tablespoons of concentrated brown gravy. Serve immediately.

Sandwiches à la Regence

For this purpose, it is necessary to order one dozen or more of very small round or oval rolls, about the size of an egg. Cut a small piece off the top of each – about the circumference of half a crown – and remove the crumb from the inside. Then fill the rolls with the following preparation:

First shred the white meat from the breast of a roast fowl, and put this in a basin. Then shred the fillets of six washed anchovies, and some red tongue or dressed ham in equal proportion to the fowl, and place these with the roast fowl. Add about ⅛ of a whole Indian gherkin or mango, also finely shredded. Season with a little chopped tarragon and chervil, and add sufficient rémoulade sauce to moisten the whole.

Once the filling has been added, cover the rolls with the cut circular pieces, and dish up on a napkin.

Note: These sandwiches may also be prepared with lobster – in which case, neither ham nor tongue should be used.

Mayonnaise of Fillets of Soles

Trim the fillets of three soles, then simmer in a sauté pan with 2 oz of butter, lemon juice, and a seasoning of salt and pepper. When done, press them between earthen dishes. As soon as they are cold, divide each fillet into 3 scallops, trim the ends, then put them into a basin with a little oil, vinegar, salt and pepper, and let them steep in this.

Next prepare an aspic border mould. Pound some rough ice into fine pieces, put it into a deep pan, then partially imbed the mould in this. Pour a small quantity of aspic jelly in the bottom of the mould, to the depth of about ⅛ inch, then cover it with a decoration, made as follows:

Cut some black truffles and boiled egg whites into very thin slices. Stamp out into the form of rings, diamonds, leaves, and so on, then arrange them with taste on the surface of the jelly. When complete, the decoration must be covered with a spoonful of aspic jelly, poured over with great care so as not to disturb it. As soon as this has set, fill the mould up with aspic. Allow this to set, then turn the border out of the mould on its dish. Fill the centre with the fillets of soles (previously drained on a napkin), neatly piled up in a conical form. Pour over some green mayonnaise sauce, garnish the base of the fillets with a neat border of trimmed prawn tails, and crown the mayonnaise with the white heart of a cabbage lettuce, stuck into half a hard-boiled egg.

Note: Fillets of turbot, salmon, trout, mackerel or gurnets may be used in place of sole. The sauce can be varied according to Nos. 97 and 99, and the base of the fillets may also be garnished with cut plovers' eggs, crayfish tails, or quarters of the white hearts of cabbage-lettuces. Some shredded lettuce, seasoned with oil, vinegar, salt and pepper, may first be placed at the bottom of the aspic border to pole the fillets on.

Princess Fritters

This kind of fritter is prepared from the remains of brioche, baba or savarin. First cut up into slices ¼ inch thick, then cut out small, circular shapes using a tin-cutter with the diameter of a five-shilling piece. Place these in a sauté pan, previously strewn with orange sugar, and pour over them sufficient cream to cover. Shake some more orange sugar over the entire surface and, just before frying the fritters, dip each one separately in very light and delicately made frying batter. When the fritters are fried crisp, let them be brightly glazed with sifted sugar and the red-hot salamander. Dish them up, pour some apricot jam, diluted with a little orange flower water, round the base, and serve.

Mince Meat à la Royale

To equal proportions of roast beef, raisins, currants, suet, candied citron, orange, lemon, spices and sugar, add a proportionate weight of stewed pears and preserved ginger, the grated rind of 3 dozen oranges and lemons, and also their juice, 1 bottle of old rum, 1 bottle of brandy, and 2 bottles of old port.

Fish

Filet de Merluche Saint-Germain

For the sauce:

4 oz butter

2 egg yolks

1 shallot, chopped

6 peppercorns

salt

1 tablespoon white stock

2 tablespoons tarragon vinegar

1 tablespoon tarragon, finely chopped

Grill the fillets and serve with béarnaise sauce, made as follows:

Put the tarragon vinegar, chopped shallot and peppercorns into a pan over a brisk heat and reduce by half. Strain into a clean bowl and add stock and the beaten yolks. Pour into a double boiler, heat and whisk continuously until it thickens like custard. Now remove from the heat and beat in the butter in small lumps, waiting for 1 lump to melt before adding the next. Finally, add the chopped tarragon and salt to taste.

Filet de Sole Veronique

sole fillets
white wine
1 onion, minced
1 lemon
butter
parsley
chilled white grapes,
     skinned and stoned
seasoning

Beat the fillets lightly, then fold and season. Arrange them in a little white wine in a buttered earthenware dish in readiness for cooking.

Put the bones and some of the trimmings of the sole in a pan with a tablespoon each of white wine and water. Add 1 small teaspoon of minced onion, some parsley stalks and a good squeeze of lemon juice. Boil for about 1 minute, then strain the liquid over the fillets. Poach the fillets gently.

When the fillets are cooked, drain them carefully and reduce the liquid until it resembles syrup. Now mix thoroughly with 1 ½ oz of melted butter.

Arrange the fillets around the dish in which they were poached and pour the buttered liquid over them, leaving them exposed until the coating has glazed. Arrange a pyramid of chilled grapes in the centre of the dish, cover immediately and serve at once.

Goujonettes de Sole

sole fillets
eggs
bread crumbs

For the sauce:
1 pint oil
3 egg yolks
1 dessertspoon tarragon
vinegar or lemon juice
pinch white pepper
⅙ oz salt

With a sharp knife slice the fillets into strips slightly less than the width of the little finger. Brush well with egg, then coat with bread crumbs and fry in deep hot fat until very crisp. Remove and drain thoroughly until dry.

To make the sauce (preferably at least 2 hours before use):

Put the egg yolks into a mixing bowl and add salt and pepper. Beating steadily all the time, add the oil drop by drop. When the sauce begins to thicken, add the oil at a faster rate. When it is really stiff, add a few drops of vinegar or lemon juice, still beating steadily. As with the oil, add increasingly quickly until all has been used. Now stir in 2 dessert spoons of boiling water to maintain the consistency of the sauce and ensure that it keeps well while standing.

Scampi Frit Sauce Mayonnaise

Dip the scampi in egg,
coat with bread crumbs and fry
in hot fat. Serve with sauce
mayonnaise, made
as follows:

2 large egg yolks
½ pint olive oil
½ teaspoon French mustard
2-3 tablespoons wine
    vinegar
white pepper and seasoning

Sprinkle the mustard over the bottom of a mixing bowl. Drop in the yolk and whisk lightly. Pour on the oil drop by drop, carefully and slowly. It is absolutely essential that there should be no pause in the whisking or stirring, and by the time all the oil has been introduced the mayonnaise will thicken until almost solid. Now season to taste with salt and white pepper. Finally, stir in sufficient vinegar to give the required consistency.

Should the mayonnaise curdle because the oil has been added too quickly, proceed as follows: Break 1 egg into a clean bowl and add the curdled mayonnaise drop by drop. The use of 2 yolks will require that more oil is added until the correct consistency is achieved. The mixture can always be thinned with a little vinegar. If the mayonnaise is to be kept for some while before using, hot vinegar should be added to ensure a smoother and whiter finish.

Suprême de Turbot Florentine

8 fillets turbot
2 lb spinach
2 oz grated cheese, Parmesan if possible
2 egg yolks
1 gill dry white wine
½ pint béchamel sauce
2 tablespoons thin cream
2–3 shallots
seasoning

Evenly butter a fireproof dish. Chop the shallots into small pieces and sprinkle them in the bottom of the dish. Lay the fillets on top and dust with salt and black pepper, then carefully pour over enough wine just to cover the fish. Cover the dish with a piece of buttered greaseproof paper and poach in a moderate oven (375°F/Gas 5) until the fish is cooked, about 20 minutes or less.

While the fish is cooking make the béchamel sauce in the usual way. Wash the spinach in several waters and cook in boiling salted water for about 10 minutes. Drain thoroughly and refresh it under the cold tap. Squeeze to remove excess moisture and reheat in a little melted butter. Season to taste and keep hot, ready to serve.

Strain off the liquor in which the fish was cooked into a pan and reduce by half over a good heat. Now add the béchamel sauce and remove from the heat. Beat the yolks with the cream and stir them into the sauce. Return to a gentle heat and stir until it thickens, not allowing it to boil. Remove from the heat and whisk in the grated cheese.

Pour a thin coating of the sauce over the bottom of a hot fireproof serving dish and cover with the spinach. Lay the fillets on top of this and add the rest of the sauce. Sprinkle with more cheese and brown under a hot grill or in the top of a hot oven for a few minutes. Serve immediately.

KIPPERS

The Queen has been partial to kippers since the war years, when she and Princess Margaret were at Windsor Castle. One day the young princesses were wandering along a dark corridor amid the 900-year-old castle's 12-foot-thick walls when a compelling aroma wafted across their path. Fascinated, they traced the smell to its source and found themselves outside the private kitchen of Mrs Alice Bruce, then housekeeper at the castle. They politely knocked on the door and were welcomed into the old-fashioned kitchen with its great iron oven range – and its frying kippers. Mrs Bruce gave the princesses their first taste of kipper, and showed them how to cook the fish as well. Kippers, in a number of uncomplicated variations, have remained a favourite with the Queen ever since – for breakfast, as a savoury or a late-night supper snack. The Queen is also fond of smoked haddock as a breakfast dish.

Soon after the Queen's coronation and her move to Buckingham Palace with Prince Philip, she had an order placed

with a firm in the Isle of Man for a weekly delivery of kippers during their season. It was arranged that a box addressed to Her Majesty the Queen, Buckingham Palace, London, should be flown in directly. The Queen once received her kippers in a rather uncustomary way, however, when Prince Philip discovered a box packed away with his clothes in his suitcase! This was while the court was at Balmoral and the Prince had been away for few days' stay with an old friend.

Soufflé au Kipper

8 oz kipper
3 eggs
¼ pint kipper stock
1 oz butter
1 tablespoon cream (optional)
½ oz flour
seasoning

Plunge the kipper in steadily boiling water and simmer until tender. Drain thoroughly and retain the stock. Flake the kipper and pound it into a paste, using a wooden spoon.

Stir the butter into the hot kipper stock to make a thick sauce. Beat into this the pounded fish and cook for 1 minute. Remove from the heat and add cream (if desired), seasoning and the egg yolks one at a time.

Whip the egg whites until stiff and lightly fold them into the mixture. Turn the mixture into a buttered soufflé dish of 1 ½ pints capacity, and level it off. Bake in a moderate oven (400°F/Gas 5) for about 30 minutes.

Délice de Sole d'Antin

8 fillets sole
4 oz button mushrooms
½ pint dry white wine
1-1 ½ oz butter
1 onion, sliced
1 carrot, sliced
2 tablespoons parsley,
    finely chopped
juice ½ lemon
bouquet garni
Hollandaise sauce
1 tablespoon tomato purée
seasoning

For the hollandaise sauce:
8 oz butter
4 egg yolks
2 tablespoonfuls water
2 tablespoons stock (fish)
2 tablespoons lemon juice
1 teaspoon tomato purée
pepper to season

First wash and thoroughly dry the fillets of sole. Fold the ends under and place in a lightly buttered fireproof dish. Evenly distribute the sliced vegetables around the sides, then add the bouquet garni and season well.

Pour the wine over carefully and cover with buttered greaseproof paper. Poach in a moderate oven (350°F/Gas 4) for about 15-20 minutes. While the sole fillets are cooking, dab the mushrooms clean with a cloth, then slice and place them in a small pan with butter, lemon juice and seasoning. Cover with greaseproof paper and the lid, and cook over a gentle heat until the mushrooms are cooked, which should take about 5 minutes. During cooking, the mushrooms should be repeatedly shaken and then be kept hot.

To make the Hollandaise Sauce:
Pour the stock into a pan and heat until reduced by half. Now stir in the water and 1 teaspoonful of tomato purée and strain on to the beaten egg yolks. Return to the heat, either in a double boiler or in a bowl standing in hot water in a larger bowl. Whisk continuously until it has become like thick, creamy custard. Remove from the heat and whisk in the butter bit by bit, only introducing another knob of butter when the previous one has melted. Finish by stirring in the lemon juice and pepper.

Now add the sauce to the mushrooms and finely chopped parsley, and ensure it is kept hot while the cooking of the fish is completed. When the fish is cooled, remove it from the oven, and drain. Strain the cooking liquor into a clean pan and keep hot over a good heat, reducing it quickly until only 2 tablespoonfuls remain. Add this to the sauce. Lay out the fillets in a hot serving dish, pour the sauce over carefully and put under a very hot grill until the top is lightly browned. Great care should be taken to ensure the subjection to intense heat is short and sharp otherwise the sauce will boil and curdle.

Blanchailles Diablées

1 lb whitebait
1 gill milk
4 oz flour
Cayenne pepper
1 teaspoon dry mustard
salt

Make sure the whitebait are thoroughly cleaned. Dip them first in milk and then in the flour seasoned with the mustard. Put the fish into a frying basket and shake until all excess flour is sifted out. Fry in deep and very hot fat until a light brown. Spread across absorbent paper to drain, then season with salt and cayenne pepper.

Serve the whitebait garnished with parsley and thin slices of lemon.

Filet de Sole Frits

For the frying batter:
4 oz plain flour
½ pint milk and water
(using ⅓ water)
1 egg
pinch of salt

Thoroughly dry the sole and dust very thinly with seasoned flour. Make a frying batter rather thinner than usual and dip the fish in this. Alternatively, beaten egg and bread crumbs can be used instead. Allow the excess batter to drain away, or shake off the surplus bread crumbs, as applies.

To shallow-fry the sole, ensure the fat or butter is very hot before submerging the fish. Cook steadily until brown, then turn and cook the other side. If deep fat is used, make certain it is not too hot. This could cause the outside to brown before the fish is cooked.

Drain the fish before serving.

TO MAKE THE BATTER:

Sieve the flour and salt together into a basin, break an egg into it and beat the mixture well. Gradually beat in just enough milk and water to give a stiff, smooth batter with no lumps. Allow to stand for a few minutes, then gradually beat in the remaining liquid. This mixture can be made some time before required but should be put into a refrigerator or some other extremely cool place. Just before using, give a final beating.

Truite Meunière

2 trout
2 lemons
3-4 oz butter
seasoned flour
little milk
finely chopped parsley
seasoning

Cut the fins off the trout with a sharp knife and remove the skins. Wash and dry on a clean cloth, then lay the fish in milk and, immediately afterwards, in seasoned flour.

Put half the butter in a frying pan and heat, then place the fish in it. Sprinkle with a little salt and cook until the flesh on the under-side is golden. Turn the trout carefully, making sure they do not break, and cook the other side until that, too, is golden.

Place the trout on a hot dish and keep hot. Wipe the pan with a damp cloth and drop in the rest of the butter. Heat quickly until it is golden brown, then add the strained juice of 1 lemon and the chopped parsley. Season, then pour over the fish. The dish should be tastefully garnished with thin slices of lemon cut from the second lemon.

Goujonettes de Merlans Sauce Tartare

For the sauce:
3 yolks of hard-boiled eggs
small bunch of chives or the
    tender green part (only)
    of spring onions
1 gill wine vinegar
freshly ground black pepper
½ pint olive oil
1 large tablespoon mayonnaise

Cut fillets of whiting into strips a little thinner than an average little finger. Brush with egg and coat with bread crumbs, then fry in deep hot fat. When golden and crisp remove from fat and drain thoroughly to ensure that the goujonettes are really dry.

TO MAKE THE SAUCE (SUFFICIENT FOR 9 PEOPLE):
Chop the chives finely or mince if spring onions are used. Pound the egg yolks, then work them into a smooth paste. Season with a pinch of salt and a good grinding of fresh black pepper. Now add the olive oil and vinegar, and stir into the paste until a smooth, light mixture is obtained. Add 1 teaspoon of chives or spring onions, followed by the mayonnaise and mix thoroughly. Pass through a sieve and serve cold.

Merlans Colbert

First, using a sharp knife, open up the whiting down the back. Bone, then season. Next dip in milk, then roll in flour. Thoroughly whisk several eggs with 1 dessertspoon of oil for every 2 eggs seasoned with salt and pepper. Dip the whiting in the liquid, then fry in hot fat.

Drain the fish and set them out on a long dish. Garnish the openings in their backs with butter à la maître d'hôtel and scatter grooved slices of lemon around the dish to decorate.

Sole Colbert

Using the upper side of the fish, separate the fillets from the spine, which should be broken in several pieces. Dip the sole in milk and roll in flour. Now dip it in a liquid comprising well-whisked eggs with 1 dessertspoon of oil to each 2 eggs seasoned with salt and pepper.

Fry in hot fat and roll the separated fillets back a little so that they may be quite free from the bones.

Drain on a piece of linen, remove the bones, and fill the space left with butter à la maître d'hôtel. Serve up on a very hot dish decorated with slices of lemon and sprigs of parsley.

Merlans à la Meunière

First scale the whiting, then make a few incisions in the flesh. Season, sprinkle with flour, place in a frying pan containing previously heated butter and cook. When the fish are nicely golden on both sides, set out in a long dish and sprinkle with chopped parsley and a few drops of lemon juice. Reheat the butter left from the frying, and scatter this over the fish as well.

Serve immediately while the butter is still frothy.

Salmon à la Regence

Boil a whole salmon, remove the skin, and mask it over with a strong glaze, mixed with pounded lobster-coral. Put an oval croustade of fried bread, about 3 inches high, on a dish and place the salmon on top. Pour round it regent's sauce, finished with anchovy butter and lemon juice. Garnish with alternate groups of quenelles of salmon (mixed with finely chopped truffles), large crayfish, button mushrooms, and small fillets of soles decorated with green gherkins, rolled in a spiral shape and simmered in a little butter and lemon juice. Form a decoration on the back and head of the fish with ornamented fillets of soles. Serve some of the sauce in a boat.

Slices of Salmon à la Tartare

Clean and draw a fine trout, stuff it with some quenelle forcemeat of whiting and stew it in 1 bottle of Chablis wine, a few mushrooms, parsley, green onions, thyme, peppercorns, one bay leaf and a blade of mace. When done, remove the skin, glaze and put on a dish in the hot closet until required for dishing up. Then strain the liquor in which the trout has been stewed, reduce it to a half-glaze and add some suprême sauce. Work in a pat of anchovy butter, a little cayenne pepper and lemon juice, then pour the sauce into a stew pan containing some small whiting quenelles, button mushrooms and prawn tails. Allow the whole to boil together for a few minutes, sauce the trout, and garnish round with a border of croustades of whiting quenelles, poached, bread-crumbed and fried. The centre of the dish should be filled with soft roes of mackerel tossed in a little of the sauce.

FLY-FISHING AT BALMORAL

At Balmoral there are abundant fine salmon to be caught in the glittering River Dee, which races through the royal estate. Whenever visiting, one of the Queen Mother's favourite pastimes was fly-fishing in these waters, often accompanied by Charles when he was younger.

The larders at Balmoral regularly contain salmon fresh from the Dee, as well as crabs, lobsters, crayfish and other shellfish, which have been caught locally. Most of the salmon caught by the royal family and their guests at Balmoral are put on an overnight train for London to be sold on the open market the following day. The vast majority is bought by the capital's luxury hotels, though it is not possible for them to claim 'Scotch salmon, freshly caught by Her Majesty the Queen' on their menus. However, it is customary for every successful angler and gun in the royal home party to be allowed to buy salmon game at well below market prices, with the prerequisite that every purchase is entered in the royal game book – a ritual as old as Balmoral itself. As for the game that is shot, much of this also quickly finds its way to the big London hotels or is sold to the local butcher in nearby Ballater.

Salmon à la Chambord

Take a whole salmon, and when properly cleansed, truss it in the shape of the letter 'S', as follows:

Thread a trussing needle with twine, pass it through the eyes of the fish, and fasten the jowl by tying the string under the jaw. Then pass the needle through the centre part of the body, draw the string tight, and fasten it round the extremity of the tail – the fish will then assume the desired form.

Boil the salmon in salt and water. When done, drain it on a dish, and immediately take off the whole of the skin, then put the fish to cool in the larder. In the meantime, prepare some quenelle forcemeat of whiting, part of which should be coloured with pounded lobster-coral. As soon as the salmon is cold, spread a layer of the quenelle over the whole surface of the fish, taking care to smooth it with the blade of a large knife dipped in hot water. Next ornament the salmon by laying some fillets of soles contisés (encrusted with truffles) in a slanting position across the back, fastening the ends under the belly of the salmon using the forcemeat. Mark out the head and eyes of the fish with fillets of black truffles. Then place the salmon on a buttered drainer of a fish-kettle, and cover the fish with thin layers of fat bacon. Moisten with 1 bottle of dry Champagne, garnish with a faggot of parsley, thyme and bay leaf, sliced carrot and onion. Cover the whole with buttered paper and the lid. Boil on the stove-fire, then put it in the oven or on a slow fire to simmer gently for ¾ hour. Drain the salmon, place it on a dish, and put it in the hot closet until ready to serve.

Meanwhile, strain the liquor in which the salmon has been braised, reduce to a glaze, add some espagnole or brown sauce, essence of mushrooms, a little grated nutmeg, a pat of anchovy butter, and lemon juice. Pass the sauce through a tammy into a bain-marie.

Just before sending the dish to the table, remove the layers of bacon and arrange groups of whiting quenelles,

mushrooms, truffles, large crayfish, and soft roes of mackerel around the salmon. Pour the hot sauce into the centre of the dish, and serve. Allow some of the sauce, with added truffles, mushrooms and quenelles, to be served in a boat.

Whitebait

Allow 4-8 oz of whitebait per person, the whitebait being eaten complete with heads, just as they are. Dust well in seasoned flour and cook in deep hot fat until crisp and tender. Drain well and serve with cayenne pepper, lemon and brown bread and butter.

Salmon à la Victoria

Braise a salmon in a mirepoix made with claret. When the fish is done, skin it and place it on a low croustade on a dish. Remove all grease from the mirepoix, then put one-third of it into a stew pan, boil it down to a demi-glaze and work in some brown sauce. Add a pat of anchovy butter, a good amount of lobster butter, cayenne pepper and lemon juice. Mix together well and pour the sauce over the salmon. Garnish it round with groups of crayfish tail, fried fillets of smelt and small quenelles of whiting. Serve some of the sauce in a boat, after adding a few thin scallops of lobster.

Slices of Salmon à la Tartare

Steep some slices of salmon in a dish with a little salad oil, salt and pepper, and a few sprigs of parsley. About ½ hour before dinner, place the slices of salmon on a clear gridiron rubbed over with whiting and broil them on a clear fire. When done on one side, turn them over, until both sides turn a light brown. Dish them up and serve with tartare, Cambridge or rémoulade sauce in a boat.

Haddocks à la Royale

Braise a salmon in a mirepoix made with claret. When the fish is done, skin it and place it on a low croustade on a dish. Remove all grease from the mirepoix, then put one-third of it into a stew pan, boil it down to a demi-glaze and work in some brown sauce. Add a pat of anchovy butter, a good amount of lobster butter, cayenne pepper and lemon juice. Mix together well and pour the sauce over the salmon. Garnish it round with groups of crayfish tail, fried fillets of smelt and small quenelles of whiting. Serve some of the sauce in a boat, after adding a few thin scallops of lobster. Bone and stuff two haddocks with some quenelle forcemeat of whiting, place them head-to-tail on a baking sheet, season them with a little salt and pepper, and bake. After allowing the haddocks to cool, cover them with a thin layer of quenelle forcemeat of whiting, then place on some fillets of soles contisés, in a slanting direction. Mask the heads with a little of the forcemeat, mixed with pounded lobster-coral, and form the eyes and mouth with truffles. Lay very thin layers of bacon over the haddocks, then cover with buttered paper. About ¾ hour before dinner, put the haddocks in the oven to finish baking. Just before serving, take off the paper and remove the layers of bacon, absorbing all the grease and moisture with a clean napkin. Then carefully transfer the haddocks to their dish and pour round it a Parisian sauce. Garnish with quenelles of lobster, placing a large scallop of truffle between each quenelle, and send to the table.

SHELLFISH

Soufflé de Homard

For the béchamel sauce:
2 oz butter
1 ½ oz flour
1 pint milk
1 small onion or shallot
6 peppercorns
½ carrot, ½ turnip
salt
blade of mace
bouquet of thyme, parsley
    and bay leaf

First prepare the carapaces of the lobster for use as soufflé dishes. Remove the meat, then cook the shells very carefully so that they retain their shape, drain and dry.

Now use the raw meat to make the mousseline forcemeat, which will later be used to fill the carapaces. To do this, cut the meat into small cubes and season with salt, pepper and a little nutmeg. Finely pound the meat with a pestle and mortar until it is of a paste like consistency, then gradually introduce two egg whites while continuing to pound the mixture. Strain the forcemeat through a fine sieve into a vegetable pan standing on ice, and give it a final stir with a wooden spoon. Then slowly mix in one pint of thick fresh cream.

Fill the half-carapaces with the mousseline forcemeat and very carefully wrap each half in strong buttered paper so that it overlaps the shell by 1 inch. This is to ensure that no filling overflows during cooking. The buttered paper should be carefully tied in place with string. Next place the carapaces on a tray, filled with sufficient boiling water to film the whole surface. Put the tray in a moderate oven (or in a steamer) and poach for about 20 minutes. Remove the carapaces and very carefully drain. Then cut the string and peel away the paper, which has been holding in the forcemeat.

Transfer each to a white napkin, garnish round with crisply curled parsley, and take to the table. Serve separately with a suitable sauce, such as normande, diplomat, a white wine sauce, or béchamel with lobster butter.

TO MAKE THE BÉCHAMEL SAUCE:

Gently simmer the herbs, vegetables and spices in milk for half an hour, then strain. Mix the butter and flour in a thick-bottomed saucepan, stirring constantly for 3 minutes and making sure it does not colour. Now gradually add the strained milk, stirring all the time, then continue to simmer gently for 5 minutes, never relaxing the stirring. Finally, season with salt and serve.

Crabe Sauce Rémoulade

For the sauce:
1 tablespoon capers,
    finely chopped
1 tablespoon gherkins,
    finely chopped
1 tablespoon tarragon,
    finely chopped
1 teaspoon anchovy essence
¼ pint mayonnaise sauce
1 level teaspoon Dijon mustard
seasoning

Remove the meat from a cooked crab and serve separately with sauce made as follows:

Blanch the tarragon leaves then chop finely. Make the mayonnaise in the usual way, adding the mustard (more can be added if an especially hot sauce is required). Stir in the anchovy essence and chopped tarragon, capers and gherkins. Season to taste.

Carp à la Royale

Cleanse a large-sized carp, wipe it with a clean cloth, and lay it on buttered paper. Place it on the drainer of an oval fish-kettle, and cover it entirely with quenelle forcemeat of whiting coloured with lobster-coral, smoothing the surface of the forcemeat with the blade of a knife dipped in whipped egg white. Place some fillets of soles contisés with green gherkins crosswise on the carp, leaving an inch space between each fillet – these are to be filled with forcemeat mixed with pieces of truffle and cut in the shape of small olives. Cover the whole with thin layers of fat bacon, and braise the carp in a white-wine mirepoix. When done, place it on a large oval dish, remove the layers of bacon and pour round it a génoise sauce. Garnish with a border of large quenelles of sole, half of which must be coloured with lobster-coral and the remainder with chopped and blanched parsley. Within the inner circle of quenelles, place alternate groups of prepared oysters and prawn tails. At the extremities, and on the flanks of the dish, place groups of crayfish, and send to the table.

Note: Carp are highly savoured on the Continent, especially those caught in the Rhine and Moselle. In England, carp, like tench, are seldom good, both being found to taste muddy when cooked. This is chiefly owing to their being taken from stagnant ponds. Only those caught in running streams can be expected to be free from this disagreeable peculiarity.

Before cleaning carp for dressing, it is necessary to extract an angular substance called the gallstone, which is to be found at the back of the head; if not removed, this is sure to impart a bitter taste, and render the best fish unfit for the table.

Skate à la Royale

Boil the skate until it is half done, drain it and, after allowing it to cool, cut it into pieces about 2 inches long. Place these in a basin and marinade them in oil, vinegar, salt and pepper. Twenty minutes before dinner, drain the pieces of skate on a napkin, then dip each piece in frying batter and fry them in plenty of hot hog's lard until they turn a fine colour. Dish up the skate in a pyramid shape and pour round it ravigote or poivrade sauce. Garnish with alternate groups of fried parsley and pieces of the liver, and serve.

Herrings Fried in Oatmeal

This is according to a recipe much favoured by King Edward VII. Head and tail some very fresh herrings, then clean. Split down the back and remove the entire backbone, and as many of the smaller bones that can be taken out without breaking the flesh. Dredge the herrings in oatmeal, then fry or grill.

Homard à l'Americaine

(Serves five people)

3 lobsters (weighing 1
  ¼ lb each)
2 shallots, finely chopped
4 tomatoes (seeded and
chopped) or 2 dessertspoons
tomato purée
1 ½ garlic cloves, finely
  chopped
½ pint dry white wine
½ gill heated cognac, plus a
  little extra
1 teaspoon mixed chopped
parsley and tarragon
1 teaspoon unsalted butter

To expose the meat, first remove the claws and cut the tails into sections. Split the bodies in half lengthwise, then remove and discard the little bag near the head. Reserve the tomalley, or green liver, of each lobster, and the coral, or eggs if the lobster is female. Both are required to make the sauce.

Season the lobster meat with salt and pepper, and toss the pieces in a few dessertspoons of hot olive oil over strong heat until the meat has stiffened and the shells are red. Pour away the oil.

Sprinkle the lobster with the shallots and the garlic, and simmer for a few minutes in a covered pan. Add a splash of cognac, cover again and simmer for a further 5 minutes. Add the wine, tomatoes and herbs. Keeping the pan covered, place it in a moderate oven for 20 minutes. Now transfer the lobster to a heatproof dish. Next reduce the sauce remaining in the pan to one-third of its original volume and add the liver, coral and a little unsalted butter. Cook for several minutes, stir in the rest of the unsalted butter, and adjust the seasoning with salt, pepper and cayenne pepper.

Pour the sauce over the lobster, sprinkle with ½ gill of heated cognac, set light to it and serve flaming.

Mayonnaise de Homard

Remove the meat from a medium-sized lobster. If the lobster is female, retain the coral for garnish. Divide the meat into neat pieces.

Prepare two crisp lettuces and arrange the leaves around a salad bowl. Hard-boil and slice an egg or eggs. Mix the lobster with ¼ pint of mayonnaise and remaining lettuce torn into shreds.

Pile the lobster meat lightly in the bowl, garnish with sliced egg, lettuce hearts, and lobster head and claws. Finally add the lobster-coral.

Meat

VEAL

Escalopes de Veau Viennoise

4 veal escalopes
2 hard-boiled eggs
seasoned flour
chopped parsley
4 anchovy fillets
3 beaten eggs
white breadcrumbs
juice of one lemon
seasoning
2 lemons
4 oz butter
capers
oil

Shape the escalopes neatly with a sharp knife then flatten them out with pressure from the blade. Dip them into seasoned flour to coat lightly then into a mixture of beaten eggs and 1 tablespoon of oil. Coat evenly with bread crumbs, which should be worked in gently with pressure of the palm of the hand. Now use the back of the knife to make a criss-cross pattern on each escalope.

Having prepared the escalopes, cut wafer-thin slices of lemon ready to put round the sides of the serving dish. Also cut one slice of lemon to go on each escalope, trimming off the rind with a sharp knife. Coil an anchovy fillet tightly to stand on the centre of each of these lemon slices. Sieve the yolks and very finely chop the whites of the hard-boiled eggs, then chop a generous handful of parsley.

Melt the butter in a heavy frying pan, at the same time carefully adding 2 tablespoons of oil to keep the colour clear. When all is melted, place the escalopes in the pan and cook for about 3 minutes. Turn them over and cook the other side for a similar time. Drain quickly and lay them on a hot serving dish, which must be kept hot.

Put a lemon slice with anchovy in the centre of each escalope and sprinkle a thin ring of parsley round each piece of lemon. Use the other lemon slices to decorate the border of the dish. Distribute the egg whites, egg yolks and chopped parsley in neat lines around the dish. Scatter the escalopes with capers. Now quickly reheat the butter in the pan, pour in the lemon juice, season to taste and pour over the meat. Serve piping hot.

Cote de Veau Sauté Chasseur

6 veal cutlets

1 tablespoon chopped shallots

6 mushrooms, sliced

2 teaspoons chopped tarragon
    and chervil

¾ cup white wine

1 ¼ cup thickened brown stock

1 tablespoon tomato sauce

butter

For the sauce:

1–5 large fresh or canned
    tomatoes

½ pint stock or liquid from can

1 rasher bacon

1 oz butter

½ oz flour

1 small onion

1 carrot

1 bay leaf

pinch sugar

salt and pepper

First sauté the veal chops in butter, then drain. Put the shallots and mushrooms into a frying pan, and brown for a few seconds over a fierce heat. Moisten with white wine and boil down. Now add the thickened brown stock and tomato sauce, and boil briskly for a few seconds. Stir in the chopped tarragon and chervil and a tablespoon of butter. Arrange the chops neatly on a hot serving dish and pour the sauce over them.

TO MAKE THE SAUCE:

Dice the bacon, onion and carrot and toss in hot melted butter. Make sure they do not brown. Add the tomatoes and bay leaf and simmer for 3 or 4 minutes if using canned tomatoes but rather longer if they are fresh. Blend the flour with the stock and mix in with the other ingredients. Then simmer for about 30 minutes, stirring from time to time. Rub through a sieve, add seasoning and a good pinch of sugar, and reheat.

Foie de Veau Sauté au Lard

It is most important that Foie de Veau is not overcooked otherwise it will become dry and unappetising. Slice the calf liver thinly and dip in seasoned flour.

Allowing about 1 oz lard for about 12 oz of liver, melt the lard and sauté the liver quickly on both sides.

Neck of Veal à la Royale

Trim and braise a neck of veal, then let it get partially cool in its own braise. Drain it on an earthen dish, and mask it entirely with a coating of thick and well-seasoned allemande sauce. As soon as the sauce has set, bread crumb it with a mixture of egg, bread crumbs and grated Parmesan cheese. Place on a buttered baking dish ¼ hour before dinner, and bake in the oven.

When done, dish it up, garnish round with a Toulouse ragoût, and surround the whole with a border of quenelles, decorated with truffles and large crayfish. Place a heart of sweetbread at each end of the dish. Decorate the sweetbread with pieces of the tip of a tongue that have been simmered in a little white braise, then cut into the shape of large hobnails and inserted in circular rows. Lightly glaze the crayfish lightly, then send the dish to the table.

Note: Necks of veal, either braised or roasted plain, or larded and braised, may also be served garnished with a macédoine of vegetables, jardinière, potato croquettes, mushrooms, or tomates au gratin. (In the last two cases, the neck of veal must be sauced with espagnole, poivrade, or brown Italian sauce, à la Milanaise, à la financière, and so on.)

SETTING THE MOOD

The Queen likes always to dine by candlelight, with the wall lights switched off and the light from the chandelier overhead subdued. She also likes candles for bigger dinner parties (of around 20 guests) given in the 1844 Room of the Caernarvon Suite. This beautiful room (so called because it was specially designed in that year for a visit from the Tsar of Russia) particularly lends itself to candlelight. Here the gilded embossing on the walls and ceiling catches the trembling light and glows magically. The rich hangings of the room look all the more magnificent in soft light.

Although the Caernarvon Suite, situated on the ground floor at the rear of the palace, is the preferred choice for private dinner and luncheon parties, the flamboyantly colourful Chinese Room at the palace front is also sometimes used. The Queen can enjoy particular oriental splendour in one room of the suite, thanks to George IV. During his major expansion of Buckingham Palace (at which time it became the vast building it is today, with over 600 rooms) he found he had overspent his budget. To raise much-needed cash, he sold his oriental pavilion at Brighton and moved much of

its furnishings to the palace. Later, during the reign of King George V, Queen Mary conducted a room-by-room search in the palace to see what hidden treasures she could find. She discovered quantities of rich oriental fabrics and furnishings, which she used to further beautify the Chinese Room. Rich drapes, elaborately embroidered with dragons, and shining lacquerwork added to the room's charm. Along the corridor that traverses the whole of the palace front, from the Chinese Room to the far corner, ornamental pagodas are set at intervals. These, too, come from the fantastic oriental pavilion, which George IV fashioned for himself in the long years of the Regency.

The tapestry in the Queen's study is another of the many beautifying touches for which Queen Mary was responsible. She not only dedicated herself to promoting the internal splendour of the palace, but also did much to better the living conditions of the staff. For all her majestic demeanor, Queen Mary was a warm and kindly person who went out of her way to break the stern Victorian ruling that 'servants should be neither seen nor heard'.

For smaller dinners of an official nature the State Dining Room is used – a gracious room between the Ballroom and Bow Reception Room, which overlooks the sweep of lawns towards the lake. It is filled with great oil paintings, dominated by a life-size picture of George IV in Garter robes. Next to this dining room is the Blue Dining Room, filled with walls of blue brocade and upholstered in blue satin. Leading into the Ballroom is the State Supper Room, which is used both as a supper room at state balls and as an assembly room for evening courts.

When the Queen holds a ball other than a state ball at Buckingham Palace, she and Prince Philip, members of the royal family and friends normally have dinner in the 1844 Room first, which is to the right of the great Bow Reception Room.

Noix or Cushion of Veal à la St George

Lard the trimmed part of your noix of veal with fat bacon, and prepare the noix for braising as follows:

First, on the drainer at the bottom of a large fricandeau or oval stew pan, place some sliced carrots, a head of celery, 2 onions (each pierced with a clove) and a garnished faggot. Cover the whole with thin layers of fat bacon, then put in the noix of veal. Surround it with the trimmings, and moisten with ½ bottle of sherry, or Madeira, and sufficient quantity of good stock to barely cover the veal. Cover with well-buttered white paper and set it to boil on the stove. Place the lid on the pan and put it on a slow fire (with live embers on the lid) or in the oven to braise gently for about 4 hours. Remember to baste frequently with the liquor in order to moisten the veal and glaze it a bright colour. The udder should be covered with thin layers of fat bacon to preserve its whiteness during the braising. When the noix is done, drain and glaze it, remove the layers of bacon, and dish it up.

Garnish with groups of button mushrooms, small quenelles of fowl (coloured with crayfish butter), cocks' combs and kernels, and turned truffles tossed in glaze. Surround these with a border of lambs' sweetbreads, half of which should be larded and the others cotised with tongue, placed alternately. Stick 4 silver skewers, each garnished with a large double cock's comb, a large truffle, mushroom and crayfish, into the noix. Pour over a rich Madeira sauce and serve.

Loin of Veal à la Royale

Prepare and braise a loin of veal. When done, allow it partially to cool in its own braise, then strain it on the drainer of the braising pan and absorb any grease with a clean napkin. Cover with quenelle forcemeat of veal, mixed with a little lobster-coral. Decorate the ends and centre using black truffles to create a bold design on the scarlet surface. Next place the loin of veal in a large oval braising pan with just sufficient consommé to bathe it to the depth of an inch. Then cover the loin with very thin layers of fat bacon, or a well-buttered oval covering of paper. Place in the oven or on a moderate stove-fire (with live embers on the lid) to boil or simmer gently for about ¾ hour. When done, drain the veal and remove the bacon or paper used to cover it.

Pour round it a ragoût of button mushrooms, small quenelles of fowl, cocks' combs and kernels. Garnish with a border of large truffles and crayfish, glaze the loin of veal with thin, light-coloured glaze and serve.

Note: This dish may also be decorated with ornamental skewers.

Carré d'Agneau à la Boulangère

Season the inside of a boned loin of lamb, then roll it and tie up with string. Melt 4 tablespoons of butter in a fireproof dish (preferably oval-shaped) and cook the lamb in this for 30 minutes. Now surround the meat with 3 fairly large potatoes cut into long slices and 3 medium-sized onions finely chopped and lightly fried in butter. Season the potatoes and chopped onion, drizzle with the butter remaining in the pan and finish cooking in the oven, basting frequently. Add 4 tablespoons of thickened brown gravy during the last few minutes of cooking.

Breast of Veal à la Windsor

Bone and trim a breast of veal, lay it on the table, spread the inner part at least an inch thick with quenelle forcemeat of veal or rabbit, then place some square fillets of boiled tongue lengthwise and place the veal between the fillets of tongue. Then carefully roll up the breast of veal, secure its shape using small iron skewers and string, and cover the ends with layers of fat bacon to prevent the forcemeat from escaping. Put the veal, trimmings and the usual complement of roots into an oval braising-pan. Moisten with two ladlefuls of good stock, and set it to braise gently on a slow fire. When done, drain, glaze and dish it up.

Garnish with French beans cut in diamond shapes (the beans should be boiled then dressed with a spoonful of béchamel sauce, salt, a little mignonette pepper, nutmeg, fresh butter and lemon juice). Then place a border of nicely glazed young carrots round the beans, and serve.

Remove the grease from the braise in which the veal has been done, clarify and reduce to a half-glaze. Serve separately in a sauceboat.

RIGHT ROYAL EATING

The Queen's taste in food is much simpler than is generally imagined. It is widely believed that she must be regaled with sumptuous meals whenever she sits down at the table; on the contrary, most of the royal dishes are so uncomplicated, despite all their French names, they could be prepared by most reasonably competent cooks.

Footmen who take the food to the royal table maintain that the food is the sort you would expect at a good but reasonably priced restaurant. When dining alone or with the family, the Queen and Prince Phillip generally prefer simple cooking, without any fancy treatments or elaborate sauces – though of course, being served from silver dishes does add a certain cachet.

The Queen, for instance, adores Irish Stew and has introduced several members of other visiting royal families to this dish. Other home-cooked favourites are kidneys, or kidney soup, lamb chops, pork chops, cutlets, mixed grills, fried sausages, eggs and bacon, and rissoles. The fact that a dish may be written down in the royal menu book as Cotelettes d'Agneau Jardinière doesn't necessarily mean something extravagant – it might just as accurately be called 'lamb chops and vegetables'.

MUTTON

Irish Stew

1 lb middle neck of mutton
2 lb potatoes
2 large onions
chopped parsley
salt and pepper
cold water

Wipe the meat thoroughly then cut into neat pieces and extract all the marrow from the bones. Cut the potatoes and onions into rings, then place alternate layers of meat and vegetables in a pan, finishing with a layer of potato. Add seasoning and sufficient water to half-cover. Bring to the boil and simmer gently for about 2 hours, or until the meat and potatoes are tender.

Pile the meat and some of the potatoes in the centre of a hot dish. Place the remaining potatoes at each end of the dish, then pour the gravy around and sprinkle with chopped parsley.

LAMB

Navarin d'Agneau aux Legumes

The most suitable cuts to select for navarin are the lower ribs, neck, breast and shoulders.

Cut up into cubes 1 ½ lb of lamb and cook in clarified fat until evenly brown. Season with salt, pepper and a pinch of sugar and sprinkle with 2 tablespoons of flour. Brown again, this time lightly.

Moisten the meat with 3 ¾ cups of stock or water and add a bouquet garni and ½ crushed clove of garlic. Add carrots, turnips, potatoes and mushrooms and other desired vegetables that are available, then cover and cook in a moderate oven for 1 hour.

Cotelettes d'Agneau

Brush each chop with a film of melted butter. Place the chops on to a grill pan and put under a red-hot grill. After about 5-7 minutes, turn the chops, lightly brush the upper sides with butter and repeat the grilling.

If desired, each chop may be served up topped with a pat of savoury butter.

TO MAKE GARLIC BUTTER:
Crush ½ clove of garlic into a little salt, then chop small. Soften 1 oz butter and knead in the chopped garlic. Divide into portions as required and leave to harden.

Carré d'Agneau Sauce Menthe

For the mint sauce:
2 tablespoon chopped mint
1 tablespoon sugar
1 tablespoon boiling water
1 ½ tablespoons vinegar

First wipe the meat with a cloth that has been wrung out in cold water and trim if necessary. Place in a tin and spread with fat or dripping. Cook the meat in a hot oven (425°F/Gas 7) for the first ½ hour, then reduce the temperature a little and complete the cooking. Baste the joint repeatedly during cooking. Allow 20-25 minutes' cooking time per lb of meat plus about 25 minutes.

TO MAKE MINT SAUCE:

Strip the mint leaves from the stalks and chop finely. Dissolve the sugar in the boiling water in a sauceboat, then add chopped mint and thoroughly stir in the vinegar to taste.

Rolled Breast of Veal à la Royale

For this preparation, follow the directions given for Loin of Veal à la Royale.

Note: After being either roasted or braised, breast of veal may also be garnished with a jardinière or macédoine of vegetables, with stewed peas, or with ragoût à la Claremont, à la Toulouse, à la Chipolata, and so on, according to convenience or fancy.

Cotelettes d'Agneau sur le Grille

Make it clear to your butcher that you want cutlets and not chops. If you can get them, cutlets from a half grown lamb are best. Very carefully trim off all the gristle and superfluous fat, shaping the cutlet neatly. Dust the cutlets with salt and pepper and lightly brush with olive oil. Grill for about 2 ½ minutes on each side, or longer if they are really big cutlets.

BEEF

READY TO ROAST

Traditionally the royal Sunday lunch of roast beef and Yorkshire pudding, with all the usual trimmings, has been a regular house favourite and was unquestionably Prince Charles's preferred meal.

One the most intriguing rooms in Balmoral Castle is the meat and game larder, down in the cold stone basement. Along one wall is a row of huge refrigerators, in which are stored all manner of joints as well as plucked and cleaned birds from the many shoots held at Balmoral during the royal season. When stocked, the larder will also include grouse and ptarmigan, two or more stag carcasses being hung, and York hams soaking in tanks. There is also another big glass tank filled with fresh flowing water and spotted trout from Loch Muick.

Braised Fillet of Beef à la Royale

Closely lard a thick fillet of beef, then daub or interlard it with small square fillets of lean ham, fat bacon and truffles. Prepare it for braising with the trimmings and usual quantity of vegetables, 1 or 2 carcases of game, and moisten with a bottle of Madeira. Set the fillet to simmer gently on a slow fire in the usual way, carefully basting it occasionally with its liquor. When done, glaze it brightly, and afterwards dish it up. Strain off the braise, clarify and reduce it, then garnish the fillet with a financière ragoût. Place round it a border of large crayfish, whole truffles and cocks' combs, and serve.

Cottage Pie de Boeuf Braisé

¾ lb chopped and coarsely
  minced cold braised beef
  from which fat and skin
  have been carefully removed
1 onion, finely chopped
½ oz dripping
¼ pint good gravy or thin tomato
  sauce (more if required)
seasoning
1 teaspoon flour

The top:
¾ lb freshly boiled potatoes
butter
hot milk
seasoning

Purée the potatoes until they are light, white and creamy. Heat the dripping in a saucepan, then add the chopped onion, cover and allow to soften slowly. Now add flour, allow it to colour, then pour on the gravy. Bring to a boil, season and simmer for a few minutes. Remove from the heat and mix in the meat. Add more gravy, if necessary, to ensure that the meat is well moistened.

Put into a pie dish and lay the potatoes on top, leaving a rough surface. Dot with small knobs of butter and bake quickly in a hot oven. When brown and crusty, remove and serve.

Braised Roll of Beef à la Royale

Prepare and braise the roll of beef. After trimming and glazing the roll, place it on a dish, and sauce it with a rich ragoût à la financière. Garnish with a border of larded lambs' sweetbreads and whole truffles, placed alternately round the dish. Ornament the roll of beef by inserting six silver skewers, garnished as follows:

Run the point of the skewer through a large double cock's comb, then a large mushroom, a fine truffle, and finally a fine crayfish. Use them to ornament the beef, and serve.

Bubble and Squeak

Cut some slices (not too thin) of cold boiled round, or edge-bone, of salt beef and trim them neatly. Also trim an equal number of pieces of the white fat of the beef, and set them aside on a plate. Boil 2 summer or Savoy cabbages, remove the stalks, chop them finely, and put them into a stew pan with 4 oz of fresh butter and 1 oz of glaze. Season with pepper and salt. Just before serving, fry the slices of beef in a sauté or frying pan, starting with the pieces of fat. Stir the cabbage on the fire until quite hot, then pile it up in the centre of the dish. Place the slices of beef and pieces of fat round it, pour a little thin brown sauce over the whole, and serve.

Braised Roll of Beef à la Windsor

Braise the roll of beef until perfectly tender, trim, glaze, and place it on a dish. Garnish round with alternate groups of stewed peas and potatoes — turned in the shape of large olives and fried in butter until a fine light colour. Clarify and reduce the braise in which the beef has been done, then use it to sauce round the beef, reserving part to be served in a sauceboat.

STEAK FOR A ROYAL BLACK EYE

The kitchen staff who were at Windsor when the Queen came to the throne will never forget one particular rush order received after a morning ride by the Queen and Prince Philip. It was for a big piece of raw steak — not for an extra nutritious royal breakfast but to treat the Queen's black eye! Later she laughingly explained, 'No, it is not true that Philip beats his wife. If you must know, my horse tossed its head and hit me.' Which is exactly what happened; Trustful, her favorite mount at the time, unexpectedly jerked his head when troubled by a fly, and the Queen had a royal black eye before she knew what had hit her.

STEAK

Rumpsteak Grillé Béarnaise

For the béarnaise sauce:
2 egg yolks
4 oz butter
2 tablespoon white stock
6 peppercorns
1 shallot, chopped
1 tablespoon finely chopped
tarragon
salt

Brush the slices of steak with plenty of oil or butter, then make sure the grill is really hot before cooking the steak. Cook quickly, turning regularly so that each side receives 2-3 minutes grilling, or longer, according to how well done the steaks are required to be.

TO MAKE THE BÉARNAISE SAUCE:
Put the vinegar, peppercorns and shallot into a pan over a good heat and reduce by half. Strain into a bowl, then add the stock and the beaten yolks. Place in a double boiler and whisk continuously until it becomes thick and like custard, then remove from the heat. Now beat in the butter a small wedge at a time, ensuring each has melted before the next is added. Add the chopped tarragon, then salt to taste.

Filet de Boeuf Montmorency

First smear the fillet with lard then poêlé it, which is done as follows:

Using a deep and thick dish, place the meat (well seasoned) on a layer of raw matignon. To make this, finely mince the red parts only of 2 medium carrots and 2 sticks of celery from near the heart. Add 1 tablespoon of raw lean ham, which has been cut into triangles, a sprig of thyme and ½ bay leaf, crushed. Drizzle liberally with melted butter, cover and cook gently in a moderate oven. Sprinkle with melted butter frequently during the cooking and glaze just before dishing up. Serve on a long dish.

TO MAKE THE MEAT GLAZE:

First reduce brown stock in a large stew pan. When it has been substantially reduced, strain it through muslin into a smaller pan. When again greatly reduced, repeat the process into a smaller pan. Continue this process with progressively smaller pans until the glaze leaves an even veneer on a withdrawn spoon. The heat should be decreased gradually during the process until it is no more than moderate for the final phase.

Serve up the glaze separately with a Madeira sauce, finished with the poêling liquor of the fillet. To this add (per pint of the sauce) 3 tablespoons of redcurrant jelly, 2 tablespoons of finely grated horseradish, and 30 moderately sweetened cherries, which have been soaking in tepid water for about 5 minutes beforehand. The cherries should be drained just before being added to the sauce.

TO MAKE THE MADEIRA SAUCE:

Reduce 1½ pints of half-glaze in a sauté pan over a brisk heat. When it has reached a stiff consistency, remove from the heat and add ⅕ pint of Madeira. Strain and keep it warm, ensuring it is not allowed to boil.

Tournedos Grillés

First lightly sprinkle both sides of the tournedos with salt, then brush with melted butter. Cook under a grill or broil in a preheated broiling oven for between 2-5 minutes, according to requirements of taste. Serve on pieces of toast, which have been sautéed in butter with accompanying artichoke bottoms and a sauce – béarnaise, Madeira mushroom, or marchand de vin are recommended.

BEEF AND STEAK

Tournedos Sautés

A tournedos is a small round thick cut from a fillet of beef and sautéed or grilled. Season well with salt and pepper 6 tournedos, which should be less than 1 ½ inches thick. Heat enough clarified butter to cover the bottom of the pan generously. Lay the steaks side by side and brown both sides for between 2-5 minutes over a high heat. Adjust the cooking time according to the thickness of the tournedos and requirements of taste – rare medium or well done. Transfer to a hot serving dish.

Pour ¼ - ½ cup of stock or red wine into the pan and cook, stirring in all the brown bits left from the steak. When the liquid has reduced by half, swirl in 1 tablespoon of butter. Pour the sauce over the meat and serve.

PIES

Veal & Ham Pie

1 lb fillet veal

6 oz ham

1–2 hard-boiled eggs

12 oz raised pastry

7 tablespoons water or
    bone stock

½ level teaspoon meat extract

1 level teaspoon gelatin

½ level teaspoon grated
    lemon rind

beaten egg for glazing

salt and pepper

Make the pastry and put in a warm basin until required. Use ⅔ to line a 6-inch cake tin or 1 lb loaf tin. Skin, wash and dry the meats, and cut into 1-inch cubes. Mix the cubes together well with salt, pepper and lemon rind, and put half in the pastry-lined tin. Cut the eggs into halves and place them on top of the meat. Now cover with the remaining cubes. Pour in 3 tablespoons of the water or stock and turn the top edge of pastry lining in over the meat. Dampen the pastry edges, roll out the remaining pastry and use this as a lid. Press down the edges, and make incisions at 1 ½-inch intervals with a sharp knife. Bore a hole the middle, brush with beaten egg and decorate with pastry leaves. Finally, brush all over with beaten egg and place in the centre of a moderate oven (375°F/Gas 4) for 2 ¼ hours. Remove and stand to cool. Meanwhile melt the gelatin in the remaining water or stock and stir this into the meat extract. When the gelatin mixture is just setting and the pie has just cooled, pour it into the pie through the hole and leave it to set firmly.

Mutton Pies

¾ lb lean mutton
¾ lb hot water crust
1 onion, finely chopped
stock
beaten egg
chopped parsley
salt and pepper

First make the pastry, then either arrange it small tins or shape cases around the base of a tumbler or mug. The rest of the pastry, which is to be used for the lids, should be kept warm. Cut the mutton into small pieces, mix with the onion and parsley, and add the seasoning. Moisten the mixture with stock, then fill the pastry cases with it.

Put the lids on the pies and make a neat hole in the top of each. Decorate the tops as required with pastry strips or other shapes, then brush the pies all over with a little egg. Place the pies on a baking sheet and bake in a hot oven until lightly browned and set. Finally reduce the temperature to about 400°F/Gas 6, and continue cooking for a further 45 minutes.

Chicken Pie à la Reine

Cut 2 chickens into small pieces as for fricassée. Cover the bottom of the pie dish with layers of veal and ham scallops, placed alternately. Season with chopped mushroom and parsley, salt and pepper, then add a little white sauce. Next neatly place the pieces of chicken in the dish and put plovers' eggs in the gaps. Add more seasoning and sauce, and on the top lay a few thin slices of neatly trimmed dressed ham. Cover the pie with puff pastry, decorate with pastry leaves, brush the pie all over with egg, and bake for 1 ½ hours.

A very good chicken pie may be made by substituting the plovers' eggs, mushrooms, ham and the sauce with the yolks of hard-boiled eggs, chopped parsley, bacon, a little mushroom ketchup, some common gravy, or even water.

UNLUCKY NUMBERS

Once, when the Queen was holding a small dinner party for close friends at Windsor Castle, her husband asked at the last minute if she would include Prince Andrej of Yugoslavia. Worried that that would mean sitting thirteen to a table, she instructed the staff to put a small table at the end of the dining table and to lay it for three places – setting out places for ten on the other table. A gap of just one inch was left between the two tables to ensure there was no question of 13 sitting down to one table. It appeared to work, for none of those present has since been able to attribute any ill luck to having been one of thirteen at the Queen's table.

HOW TO ENTERTAIN THE QUEEN

Just as there are set rules and protocols observed at a state banquet in Buckingham Palace, so there is a certain procedure when the Queen and Prince Philip are entertained. Wherever a royal visit is to be made, the Queen's hosts are first issued with a series of written instructions from the palace.

With respect to how the royal guests should be seated, at public lunches the host should have the Queen to his right and the Prince to his left. The next most important male guest must be seated to the right of the Queen. Under no circumstances are equerries and other members of the royal entourage to be grouped around the Queen and Prince Philip. The instruction is that they should be widely divided among the rest of the guests. For more informal meals the palace advice is: 'The Queen and Prince Philip like to sit opposite each other across the table.'

Inevitably there are one or two things the Queen and her husband do not like, and the hosts are duly warned in advance. The palace instruction states only: 'Neither the Queen nor the Duke of Edinburgh likes oysters. The Queen often drinks a glass of red or white wine with her meals as well as orange juice. His Royal Highness prefers gin and tonic or lager to Champagne before meals or during the day.'

As regards table etiquette, the palace states, 'If a Minister of the Church is present at a private luncheon or dinner party, the Queen usually asks him to say grace at the beginning of the meal.' When it comes to the royal toast: 'If it is desired to toast the Queen at a public dinner or luncheon, it is usual for the Chairman to do so informally and to include the Duke of Edinburgh. Members of the royal family do not normally respond to toasts and no toasts should be given without ample warning.'

The palace advises that an hour and a half should be allowed for an official lunch attended by the Queen, including time for her to meet local dignitaries and sign the visitors' book. A special request is that 'If possible presentations should not exceed 20 people'. Also all presents offered to the Queen by private individuals, apart from personal friends, must be refused. There are a few exceptions to the rule, one of these being 'food – if perishable'.

Whenever the Queen and Prince Philip make a joint tour they prefer a simple lunch together, should official duties permit, as invariably they have dinner engagements in the evening.

After 12 years of cooking for the royal family when travelling aboard trains, British Railways' head chef, Charles Mellis, says, 'Cooking for them is no trouble at all – they like plain, regular diets and mustn't be overloaded with heavy food.' He would study the court circulars in advance of a royal train trip to get an idea what they had been doing and eating before he fed them. He would then submit two menus 'with no frills', written in French, to Buckingham Palace for final selection. 'I always took into account the fact that appetites vary according to the sort of mental and physical exercises a person has been taking,' explains Mr Mellis. 'The Queen has an ordinary appetite and likes roast lamb and beef. Her only dislike I know of is grapefruit.'

When making a long flight for a state visit abroad, the Queen and her husband usually have rather more elaborate, though still fairly light meals. A typical royal flight menu is: smoked Scottish salmon and Cornish lobster, grilled fillet of beef maitre d'hotel, accompanied by buttered French beans, a macédoine of vegetables, fried potatoes and salad, followed by vanilla cream parfait, cheese and cream crackers, celery hearts, fresh fruit and coffee.

Poultry and Game

CHICKEN

Poulet au Riz

1 plump chicken
1 lemon
1 stick celery
1 clove garlic
1 cup cream
herbs (or bouquet garni)
neck and giblets of chicken
    (optional)
2 oz butter
1 carrot
1 onion stuck with a clove
2 sprigs tarragon
salt and pepper

Rub the chicken with the juice of the lemon and a small quantity of salt. Inside the bird put the butter, a piece of lemon peel, a sprig of tarragon, salt and pepper. Place the chicken in a deep pan with the celery, carrot and onion and cover with water. If desired, also include the neck and giblets.

Put the lid on the pan and cook over a medium heat. This should not take longer than 45 minutes if the bird is tender. About 20 minutes before the chicken is expected to be ready, remove the celery, onion and carrot (and neck and giblets if they were included) and pour the rice into the pan – allow about 2 oz per person. The rice must cool fairly fast during the final 20 minutes the chicken is over the heat.

Poulet Rôti

Rub the chicken with lemon juice and season with salt and pepper both inside and out. Put a big lump of butter and a thick piece of lemon peel inside the bird, then cover it securely with well-buttered greaseproof paper. An even tastier option, in place of the butter and lemon peel, is a piece of bread crisply fried in butter and rubbed with garlic. Place the bird on its side in a roasting dish and surround it liberally with butter.

Put into a moderately heated oven (325–350°F/Gas 3-4) and cook for 15 minutes. Now turn the bird over, ensuring that the butter is not becoming burnt. Turn the oven down a little and cook for a further 15 minutes, then remove the greaseproof paper and return the chicken to the oven, this time breast uppermost. Baste generously, using additional butter if necessary, then cook for another 15 minutes, or until the bird is a rich golden brown.

Pour the gravy from the pan into a gravy boat and serve with the roast chicken. In addition, serve melted butter flavoured with lemon juice or tarragon leaves.

ALTERNATIVE METHOD WITH FORCEMEAT STUFFING:

Stuff the bird from the neck end with good forcemeat stuffing, ensuring that it is not too tightly stuffed because the forcemeat expands with cooking. Slit at the tail end, in such a way that the parson's nose can be pushed through, and secure the neck under the wings. To improve the shape further, pass string through one wing and leg, through the body to the other leg and wing. Cross the string underneath, draw up and tie to pull the various limbs into a neat shape.

Place the bird in a tin containing a liberal amount of dripping, then cook in a hot oven (425°F/Gas 7) for 1-1 ½ hours according to size. Baste frequently and ensure that the flesh is not permitted to dry. About 10-15 minutes before the roasting is complete, take off the covering so that the breast can cook a golden brown. Cut and remove the string, garnish with watercress and serve accompanied by chipolatas, bacon-and-mushroom rolls and bread sauce.

Grilled Chicken

1 small chicken (broiler)
4 tablespoons cooking oil
1 tablespoon lemon juice
salt and pepper
green salad

Cut the chicken into 4 even joints, 2 comprising the legs and surrounding meaty sections and 2 comprising the wings and breast. Place them in a grill pan. Mix the oil, lemon juice and seasoning together and pour over the chicken joints. Leave to stand for about 2 hours, turning occasionally. Cook under a medium grill for about 20 minutes, turning regularly and basting with the oil mixture.

Serve poured over with the juices from the grill pan and a crisp green salad on a side plate.

Curry de Poulet

1 boiling fowl
1 onion
1 skinned tomato, sliced
1 chopped apple
½ oz flour
1 oz dripping
1 dessertspoon chutney
1 oz curry powder
lemon juice
boiled rice

Cut the chicken into joints, allowing as far as possible one joint per person. Stew gently for 2-3 hours or until tender. Chop and fry the onion in the dripping until golden, then add the chicken and apple. Remove the joints of chicken after a few minutes, ensuring they are kept hot. Meanwhile add the curry powder and flour and fry for 2-3 minutes. Now pour in ¾ pint of the chicken stock and bring to the boil. Add the chutney, tomato and a liberal squeeze of lemon juice. Simmer gently for about 20 minutes.

The chicken should be served up on a hot dish with the curry sauce poured over, and surrounded by a good ring of rice.

Poularde Froide

Truss the chicken and cover the breast with rashers of fat bacon. Roast in the oven, adjusting the cooking time according to size – allow 25 minutes for a 3 lb bird. Remove the bacon and stand in a cool larder to become completely cold, when it will be ready for serving.

Poussin Rôti
(Spring Chicken)

First thoroughly chop the chicken liver and season it well with salt, pepper and a little grated nutmeg. Place this inside the bird along with a bouquet garni and a spoonful of butter. Now truss the chicken, lard with bacon fat and put it on the spit. Cook over a strong heat, basting frequently. When the bird is three-quarters cooked, sprinkle with fresh bread crumbs and complete cooking when richly browned. Serve with its own juices, which should be separate in a gravy boat.

Poussin Poêlé aux Nouilles

Boil the noodles in salted water until half-cooked, then drain well. Toss them in melted butter and finely grated cheese. Now stuff the poussin with the noodles, place in a covered earthenware dish with butter and cook in the oven. When done transfer it to a warmed dish and keep hot.

The pan juice should be diluted with ½ cup of white wine and thickened rich brown veal gravy. Stir in 1 teaspoon of tomato purée, pour the sauce over the poussin and serve immediately.

Poussin Poêlé à la Derby

Cook the rice in butter and mix with truffles that have been cut in large dice. Stuff the poussin with this mixture, cover and cook in the oven. Next cook 8 large truffles in port wine and sauté 8 slices of foie gras in butter. Place them around the poussin and pour over it the cooking juices diluted with the port wine and thickened rich brown veal gravy.

DUCK

Canard Sauvage Rôti

(Serves 6-7 people)

3 wild duck, about 2 ½ lb each
3 dessertspoons cognac
9 celery stalks, with leaves

Ensure that the duck are thoroughly plucked and cleaned. Singe by passing over a flame and remove any remaining pinfeathers with tweezers. Wipe the birds, both inside and out, with a clean damp cloth. Sprinkle with salt and pepper, and brush with a liberal coating of melted butter. Dust the breasts with flour and place three stalks of celery into each duck. Truss them lightly with string.

Place the duck in a very hot oven (475°F / Gas 9) and roast for about 20 minutes. Remove them from the oven and allow them to stand for 10 minutes before serving, to allow them to retain their natural juices. Then cut the ducks into quarters and arrange upon a hot serving dish.

Pour the juices that run out during carving into the gravy in the roasting pan, stir in the cognac, and heat almost to boiling point. Season as required and pour over the duck.

CHRISTMAS AND TRADITIONAL CELEBRATIONS

The royal family and their staff always celebrate the festive season in old-fashioned style, beginning with staff balls at both Windsor Castle and Buckingham Palace, which are attended by as many members of the royal family as can be arranged. The palace ball is the social function of the year for the royal household, a grand affair that takes place in the magnificent palace Ballroom, measuring 122 feet long and 60 feet wide. The castle ball is held in the splendid Waterloo Chamber, with the adjacent St George's Hall used for the lavish running buffet. On such occasions it is tradition for the staff to receive a wonderful selection of Christmas presents from the Queen.

However, Christmas is not the only time that the royal family include their staff in celebrations. At royal weddings, royal births, and other happy events, the staff is always remembered. One of the customary ways is for a bottle of very good vintage port to be sent round to each department of the household 'to drink a toast with Her Majesty'. In some departments a variation of the system was devised to make the event special for one member of the staff in particular; names

go in a hat and a bottle of port is raffled.

It was at one of the staff balls soon after the end of the Second World War that an especially amusing interchange took place between the Queen and an 'unofficial' guest. King George VI and his wife Queen Elizabeth, followed by Princess Elizabeth, Prince Philip and Princess Margaret, had entered the ballroom and were moving among the household staff and their guests (each member of staff can invite a guest to such occasions). Most of the guests were hoping that some member of the royal family would single them out for a few words. The Queen walked straight up to a young man standing near the bar who appeared as though he would rather escape royal notice – which was understandable, as he was not a relative of any of the household staff but was in fact a newspaper seller from nearby Victoria Station. The royal servant, who had taken a chance by inviting him, had assured the newspaper seller he was not likely to be questioned by anyone, and now the Queen herself was heading towards him. In a panic, he tried to recollect what he had heard her ask other guests. Mostly it had been along the lines of, 'And where do you come from?' as

she addressed long-retired royal servants now living in grace-and-favour residences at Hampton Court and Windsor. The last person the Queen addressed had replied, 'Windsor Castle, ma'am'. Then, turning to the nervous newspaper seller, the Queen asked, 'And where do you come from?' 'Elephant and Castle, ma'am,' he blurted out, being the first thing that entered his head. The Queen smiled graciously, wished him a happy evening, and moved on. But in the royal suite, and royal household, later that evening there was much laughter as the story went the rounds.

Since the days of King Edward VII, it has been customary for the royal Christmas to be celebrated at the 'big house' at Sandringham, as Edward made his home there during the many years he was Prince of Wales in the long reign of Queen Victoria. However, in recent years the Queen and her family have spent the holiday at Windsor Castle, because this has always been her favourite home — understandably so, since, apart from its historic and fascinating atmosphere, it is also the place where she spent so much of her childhood. Christmas fare at Windsor is the same and just as good as at Sandringham, the staff, royal family and guests all enjoying roast Norfolk turkey with chestnuts, herb stuffing and cranberry sauce, followed by Christmas pudding with brandy sauce.

Of all the festive-season memories for the royal family, an incident involving the Queen Mother at Sandringham must be among their fondest. The old year was drawing to an end (it was traditional to stay on at Sandringham until at least the second week in January) and the Queen Mother, in the midst of a happy family party, had been blindfolded as midnight approached. Prepared to kiss the first member of the royal party she caught, she heard a sound behind her that she took to be one of her fellow party guests. In actual fact it was the French windows leading out to the lawn, which had gently opened and shut. At once the Queen Mother groped her way towards the sound, enveloped a shrinking figure in her arms, felt for the face, and kissed him. A shriek of laughter greeted her warm salutation. She plucked off her blindfold only to discover the blushing footman she had just embraced! The Queen Mother laughed louder than anyone, and the footman soon recovered from his embarrassment as he joined them all in a glass of punch to toast the New Year.

TURKEY

Dinde Rôtie Palace

For the sausage-meat stuffing:
1 lb pork sausage meat
1 large onion, chopped
4 tablespoons fresh bread crumbs
1 oz dripping
½ teaspoon mixed herbs
1 teaspoon chopped parsley
seasoning

Cranberry Sauce:
8–12 oz cranberries
2–3 oz sugar
¼ pint water
butter

Stuff the turkey with sausage-meat stuffing (see below). Take care not to stuff the bird too full because the stuffing swells during cooking and could burst the skin. Cover the breast with rashers of fat bacon and cook in a moderately hot oven (275°F/Gas 5) allowing 15 minutes per lb weight (after dressing). Baste frequently during cooking and when the breast is a rich brown cover loosely with a sheet of foil or greaseproof paper.

Carve the turkey and serve well garnished with whole chestnuts, which have been coated with sausage meat, dipped in egg and breadcrumbs and deep-fried. Also include slices of stuffing, cranberry sauce and jus.

TO MAKE SAUSAGE-MEAT STUFFING:
Thoroughly mix the onion with the sausage meat then sauté in the dripping for a few minutes. Mix in the other ingredients.

Simmer the cranberries in the water until done, strain through a sieve, then stir in sugar to taste and a knob of butter. An unsieved sauce can be made with a syrup of water and sugar. Drop in the cranberries and cook until thick, then add butter.

GAME

Perdreau Rôti Froid et Jambon

Roast the partridge in a moderately hot oven for about ¾ hour. To ensure that the flesh does not dry and lose flavour, cover the breast with fat bacon and baste liberally during cooking. Remove the bacon towards the end of cooking and dredge the breast with a little flour. Now and again baste the bird and return to the oven until nicely brown.

The partridge should be served cold with slices of lean ham.

Grouse à la Crème

Wrap rashers of fatty bacon around a good plump grouse and truss it neatly. Melt a large tablespoonful of butter in an earthenware casserole, then add the grouse. When the bird has been well browned in the butter, place the casserole (uncovered) into a hot oven (425°F/Gas 7) for about 20 minutes, basting frequently. Remove the bird from the casserole, cut and remove the string and with it the larding bacon. Replace the grouse in the casserole and pour over it ½ cup of fresh thick cream. Put it back into a slow oven (325°F/Gas 3) and baste frequently for the remainder of the cooking.

Faisans Poêlés aux Céleris Sauce Suprême

For the sauce suprême:
1 pint sauce velouté (basic sauce)
1 gill thick cream
4 egg yolks
1 ½ oz butter
seasoning

Place the pheasant with butter in a covered casserole and cook in the oven. When done, set on a hot serving dish and surround with braised quartered celery hearts. Finally pour over the sauce suprême and serve.

TO MAKE THE SAUCE SUPRÊME:

First make the basic sauce with 2 ½ oz of butter, 2 oz of plain flour and 1 ½ pints of chicken or veal stock. Next whisk together the egg yolks and cream, then pour in a little of the hot sauce. Mix well. Now pour this into the remainder of the sauce.

Place over a gentle heat and stir continuously, without allowing it to boil, until it thickens. To test for correct consistency, coat the back of a wooden spoon with the sauce and draw a finger lightly across the surface to make a furrow. If this does not close up it is just right and the sauce should not be removed from the heat. Season if required and whisk in the butter, a knob at a time. Finally strain and serve.

THE EVER-PRESENT PHEASANT

There can be no doubt about pheasant being the favourite game dish of the Queen and Prince Philip, and when in season it appears repeatedly on the royal menu. For this reason there is always a large number of pheasants stored in the giant deep-freeze, which the Queen had installed in the palace kitchens some years ago. Previous to this, selected game and fish were sent to several deep-freeze stores in London for the palace kitchens to draw upon when required. In addition to pheasant, the Queen's chefs keep a healthy supply of game deep-frozen in readiness, as seen from this typical palace list:

55 pheasants
33 partridges
21 woodcock
20 grouse
3 snipe
sand grouse
venison
33 salmon
4 lb prawns
2 lobsters

At Balmoral and Sandringham the success of the hunting and shooting on the moors and fields always has a direct bearing on the main course for dinner, which is why grouse, venison, pheasant and partridge appear in a variety of forms with great regularity. After the court returned to London from Balmoral, the royal family would also hold regular shooting parties in Windsor Great Park.

In the days of Edward VII there were lavish supplies of hot food for the royal shooting parties, even though it was relatively simple by his standards. A typical picnic lunch might consist of mulligatawny soup and Scotch broth, stewed mutton, hashed venison, Irish stew and game pies. For dessert there would be plum pudding and apple tart.

Rissoles de Faisan

¾ lb cold cooked pheasant
¾ lb creamed potatoes
flaky pastry
bread crumbs
fat for frying
seasoning
parsley or watercress to garnish

Make sure all bones and sinews are removed from the cold pheasant, then mince finely and place in a bowl with creamed potatoes. Add the seasoning and mix well. Mould the mixture into rissoles.

Roll out the pastry very thin, then use a pastry-cutter (plain or fancy-edged) to cut out two pieces of pastry for each rissole. Fill one piece of pasty with a formed rissole and moisten the edges with water. Cover with a second piece of pastry the same shape and size and press the edges together to seal them.

Dip the rissoles in egg and breadcrumbs, put into hot fat and fry quickly on both sides. Garnish with watercress or parsley.

Chaud-Froid Brun

1 pint demi-glacé sauce
⅔ pint gelée de gibier
½ gill liquor from conserved truffles
1 sherry glass Madeira

Add the truffle liquor to the demi-glacé sauce and briskly heat the mixture. Stir constantly, adding the jelly a little at a time until all has been combined. Continue cooking until the liquor has been reduced by about one-third. Check the seasoning and add salt and pepper if necessary. Cool a little of the sauce on the back of a spoon to check whether it has acquired a suitable consistency to firmly coat the bird. If so, stir in the Madeira and strain through a cloth. Cool the sauce slowly, stirring regularly to prevent a crust forming.

Pâté de Bécasses

Completely bone the woodcock and stuff with forcemeat au gratin mixed with the chopped trimmings of the birds, truffles and pieces of foie gras. Now reshape the woodcocks and wedge them tightly side by side in an oval mould lined with pastry, which has been coated with the truffled game forcemeat and bacon rashers. Cover with a layer of forcemeat and place a rasher of bacon on top. Now cover with an oval-shaped piece of rolled-out pastry, seal, crimp the edges and decorate the top with pieces of pastry cut into decorative shapes. Bore a hole in the middle of the top and brush with beaten egg. Bake in a medium oven and, when the pie is quite cold, pour in through the hole aspic jelly based on a game fumet.

Cailles sous la Cendre

First stuff the quails with a little smooth truffled game forcemeat. Wrap each in a buttered vine leaf, then in a slice of thin bacon, and finally in double sheets of buttered paper. Secure with string. Place the quails on the hearthstone of a good log fire, which is absolutely necessary for this dish. Cover with very hot cinders and cook for 35 minutes, renewing the hot cinders the moment they begin to cool. Just before serving, remove the charred coverings of bacon and vine leaves.

Cailles Rôties sur Canapé

First wrap each quail in a thin rasher of bacon, secure with string, and roast in a hot oven for about 12 minutes. Serve each bird on a piece of evenly browned toast spread with rouennaise (poultry liver paste) and garnish with pieces of the browned fat pork.

Make the pan sauce and serve separately. Bread sauce and redcurrant jelly may also be served.

TO MAKE THE ROUENNAISE:
Heat 2 tablespoons of rendered salt pork fat until very hot. Add 1 cup of chicken or duck livers, 1 bay leaf, a pinch of thyme, 1 teaspoon of salt and a little pepper. Cook over high heat for about 4 minutes then add 3 tablespoons of cognac or sherry. Mix thoroughly, ensuring the livers are completely reduced to a paste, then rub the mixture through a fine sieve.

TO MAKE THE PAN SAUCE:
Take the cooked quails from the roasting pan and pour away the fat, but do not wash the pan. Put in 2 tablespoons butter and 1 ½ teaspoons of flour. Mix thoroughly and cook for 2 minutes. Add 1 ½ cups of double cream, stirring it in slowly, and cook until the sauce thickens, finishing with 1 teaspoon of lemon juice. Small white stoned grapes, or small canned cherries drained of their juice, may be added if desired.

Perdreau Rôti

Cover the breast of a plump partridge with strips of fat bacon to prevent the flesh drying during cooking. Place in a baking tin and roast in a moderately hot oven. Allow 15 minutes per lb plus 15 minutes. Shortly before the bird is cooked, remove the bacon, dredge the bird with flour, then baste liberally and return to the oven.

Serve the roast partridge well garnished with watercress and accompanied by a thin gravy.

Perdreaux aux Choux

2 young partridges

2 ½ lb cabbage (after removing outer leaves)

large slice fat bacon

chipolata sausages

1 large onion, stuck with clove

½ lb carrot

¾ pint stock (or ½ stock and ½ white wine)

bouquet garni

1 oz butter

1 tablespoon flour

lard

salt and pepper

Melt a little lard in a pan and when hot put in the partridges. Cook until they are lightly and evenly browned all over, then remove from the pan. While the partridges are browning, remove the leaves from a good firm cabbage and thoroughly wash and blanch. Drain well, season with salt and pepper, then put into the pan in layers on top of the slice of fat bacon.

On to this place the partridges, scraped whole carrots, sausages, onion, herbs and stock. Cover with buttered paper, then put on the lid, ensuring that it fits tightly. Simmer very gently in the oven for 1-1 ½ hours. As soon as the partridges are tender, remove them, returning them to the cabbage a few minutes before serving.

To serve, first cut the bacon into small pieces and slice the sausages. Place the cabbage in the centre of a dish, then put the partridges on the cabbage and garnish with the sausages, and so on. Over the whole pour some stock, which has been thickened with a little flour and butter.

SERVING INSTRUCTIONS – KEEPING IT HOT

Although many improvements – including effective central heating – have been carried out in Buckingham Palace since King George VI dubbed it the Ice Box, it is still a most inconvenient home. Royal meals have to be taken literally hundreds of feet along corridors and up lifts before they can be set before the Queen. After setting out on a footman-propelled mobile electric hotplate from the kitchens near the Trade Gate in the south wing of the palace, the meals have to traverse a 100-foot basement corridor running the full length of the palace front. At the far end there is a lift to the first floor, and another 50 feet at least of red-carpeted corridor before the Green Tea Room is reached. Although some of the basement walls have been knocked down to provide short-cuts through the palace's labyrinthine passages, the problem remains.

Traditionally, footmen employed in these services compete with each other to achieve a record run between kitchen and dining room, and hotplates stand warming up in the kitchens in readiness for the great dash. According to below-stairs statistics, the fastest a footman can propel a hotplate from kitchen to lift is 30 seconds, taking a further 30 seconds to travel in the lift and along the royal corridors.

Pheasant Pie

Remove any remaining flesh from a roast pheasant that has been carved. Cut into small pieces and brown in butter, adding a little cayenne pepper and salt. Remove and keep hot. Chop up 1 shallot and brown in butter, then mix it with the pheasant. Add this to as much spaghetti as required for the pie, according to its size, and mix well. Put into a pie dish and cover with flaky pastry. Bake in a hot oven for about 20 minutes, until the pastry is nicely browned.

Perdreaux Rôtis sur Canapé

Roast the birds until browned and tender. Serve a whole bird, or half if they are especially large, on toast spread with rouennaise. Garnish with pieces of browned fat pork or bacon. The pan sauce should be served separately.

Croquettes de Gibier

Dice 2 cups of finely cooked game. To this add 6 cooked mushrooms, finely chopped, and 3 tablespoons of chopped truffles. Reduce 1 cup of Madeira sauce or brown sauce until it is very thick and mix with the other ingredients. Stand to cool.

Shape the mixture into croquettes and coat them à l'anglaise. Cook them in hot deep fat until golden brown, then set them out on absorbent paper to drain them. Serve with any desired sauce.

Cailles à la Royale

This spectacular-looking dish of chaud-froid of quails served around a centrepiece of granite aux ananas should be attempted only by more experienced cooks.

To make the chaud-froid of quails, the birds should be plucked, drawn and trimmed but have their heads reserved. Bone the quails with a very small, sharp knife, ensuring the breasts remain intact. Simmer the bones and trimmings in enough water to poach the birds, producing a broth. Season lightly.

Now, using only sufficient liquid to cook them comfortably, poach the boned quails for about 10 minutes at a steady simmer. The heads should be cooked at the same time. Remove the birds and heads, drain, then stuff the quails with pâté de foie gras.

Use the cooking liquor to make a gelée de gibier (recipe following) and from this a chaud-froid brun (recipe following). Keep enough jelly in reserve to evenly gloss the completed chaud-froid. Place the birds on a grid or sieve and spoon over them an even coat of chaud-froid brun. Now arrange the quails on a serving dish on a layer of the chaud-froid brun. Decorate with a coating of gelée de gibier and little shapes of chopped sliced truffle and white of hard-boiled egg. Now, using very small sharp skewers (a toothpick is excellent for the purpose), reattach the heads to the breasts. Similarly decorate them. Artificial eyes can be made for the heads by inserting a tiny round of truffle in the centre of a little circle of white egg.

The granite aux ananas is a pineapple water ice made with a syrup prepared from fresh, ripe pineapples. It should be of a snow like consistency. Just before serving, fill the centre of the dish, around which the chaud-froid of quails is arranged, with a mound of water ice. Serve immediately.

Gelée de Gibier

7 pints of water

2 lb knuckle of veal

1 ½ lb veal bones, chopped

2 small calf's feet, blanched and
    cut in pieces

1 old chicken, cut in 4 or
    5 pieces

1 small leek

½ head of celery

¼ lb scraped, scalded pork skin

1 medium onion

2 carrots

1 bouquet garni

1 clove

½ oz salt

Fill a metal stew pan with the water, place in all the constituents and bring gently to the boil. Simmer for 6 hours, stirring and skimming at regular intervals. Remove, strain through a linen cloth and stand to cool. It is usually better to do this the day before to ensure that the cooling process is very slow.

When the liquor is well cooled the fat will collect on the surface. Most of the solid matter that has got through the strainer will collect at the bottom, making it easy to remove the fat and the other impurities from the solid jelly. Should the jelly prove to be insufficiently set, and not the firm, quick-setting aspic required for coating birds, a small quantity of leaf gelatine should be dissolved in the rewarmed jelly.

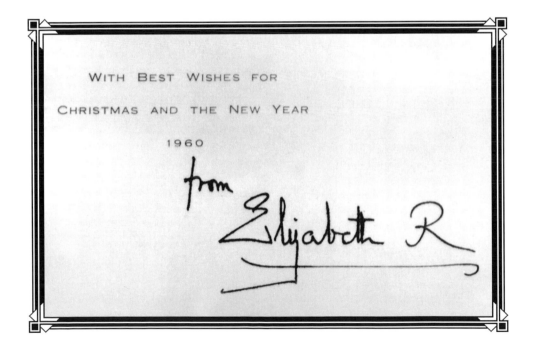

WITH BEST WISHES FOR

CHRISTMAS AND THE NEW YEAR

1960

from Elizabeth R

Croquettes de Canard Sauvage

¾ lb cold cooked wild duck

¾ lb creamed potatoes

beaten egg

bread crumbs

seasoning

fat

parsley or watercress, to garnish

Carefully extract any bones or pieces of skin from the cold cooked wild duck. Mince the flesh finely and put into a bowl with creamed potatoes and seasoning. Mix these together thoroughly, then mould croquettes from the mixture. Coat each croquette with beaten egg and roll in breadcrumbs until evenly coated all over.

Heat fat in a pan until smoke begins to rise then fry the croquettes until they are golden brown. Drain carefully and serve immediately, garnished with parsley or watercress.

Faisan en Casserole

1 pheasant

4-6 oz mushrooms, sliced

2 rashers bacon, chopped

stock

port wine (optional)

seasoned flour

fat

chopped parsley, to garnish

salt and pepper

Joint the pheasant and dip each piece in seasoned flour. Heat the fat in a frying pan and fry the pheasant sections until golden brown. Now put the meat in a casserole with the bacon, mushrooms, salt and pepper, and enough stock to half-cover the pheasant. A little port wine may be added with the stock according to taste. Cook gently in a moderate oven (350°F/Gas 4) for about 1 hour. Sprinkle the surface with chopped parsley before serving.

Vegetables

HOME-GROWN VEGETABLES

The vegetables served at the royal table have almost always been picked from the royal gardens at Windsor Castle. Although a fresh supply is delivered most mornings, there is also an emergency stock kept refrigerated.

As well as providing many of the vegetables at the palace, the market gardens in the grounds of Windsor Castle produce an abundance of fruit and flowers. It was largely due to the efforts of Prince Philip that the royal estate is now not only self-sufficient but also profitable. It supplies hundreds of boxes of mushrooms as well as large quantities of

strawberries to markets. Chestnuts are another harvest of the Windsor estates and it has long been a tradition to roast chestnuts around a glowing fire on a cold winter's night.

Although no vegetables are grown in the grounds at Buckingham Palace, it can lay claim to some magnificent mulberry trees, the eldest survivor of which was originally planted by King James I in 1609. Another of the trees is actually the offspring of William Shakespeare's famous tree from Stratford-upon-Avon.

An excellent variety of Cox's Pippins apples are grown in abundance at

Sandringham but the entire crop is sold without any being set aside for the royal family – so if the Queen wishes to sample her own produce, the royal household invariably has to buy their own.

Vegetables are much enjoyed by the royal household. The Prince has always been partial to salads, undoubtedly because of his wife's fondness for them since her childhood, and has a number of choice dishes that he will often prepare himself. Potatoes in almost any form, including chips, have been a favourite food of the royal children. The Queen also likes fried potatoes. Another popular potato dish – known to the palace as Pommes Royale – is potatoes half-fried in deep fat, drained and finished in butter, then drained again and served decorated with chopped parsley and chervil.

Choux de Bruxelles

Trim away any bruised or discoloured outer leaves from the sprouts, then with a sharp knife mark a cross on the base of each sprout. Put in boiling water and boil briskly for 10 minutes or until tender.

Petits Pois au Beurre

First cook the peas until tender, then drain and toss them over a fierce heat to dry. Add a pinch of powdered sugar, then toss with butter in a proportion of 3 oz to a pint of peas.

Potato Croquettes

Mash the potatoes so that they are both smooth and firm, then form them into croquettes and dust with a little flour. Now coat them with beaten egg and bread crumbs. Heat some fat in a deep frying pan until a faint blue haze rises, then put the croquettes carefully into frying basket. Fry briskly for several minutes and drain well before serving.

Choux-fleur Sauce Mousseline

For the sauce mousseline:

2 egg yolks

1 oz butter

cream

2 tablespoons lemon juice or
    white wine vinegar

grated nutmeg

cayenne pepper

salt and pepper

Remove all the outer leaves from the cauliflower and cut away the thick stalk. Cut up the flowered head into small sprigs, put into boiling salted water and cook rapidly. Pour over sauce mousseline and serve.

TO MAKE THE SAUCE MOUSSELINE:

Use a double saucepan or a basin standing in a larger basin of hot water. Put the egg yolks, cream, lemon juice or vinegar and seasoning into the top of the pan and whisk over hot water until the sauce begins to thicken. Drop in the butter, a small knob at a time, continuing to whisk until each has completely melted before adding the next. Immediately before serving fold in a third as much stiff-whipped cream as the quantity of sauce.

Asperges Sauce Mousseuse

For the sauce:

½ lb beure manié

2 tablespoons firm whipped
cream

lemon juice

⅓ pint cold water

salt

Cook the asparagus as above and drain well. Serve at once with the hot sauce.

TO MAKE THE SAUCE:

Put the butter into a well-cleaned and dried saucepan over heat. Season with salt and a few drops of lemon juice and whisk, meanwhile gradually adding the cold water. Finally add the cream.

Asperges Sauce Chantilly

Wash asparagus spears thoroughly and cut off the hard ends. Tie in a bundle and put into boiling salted water either in a large saucepan or in a deep baking tray if the spears are very long. Simmer very gently, otherwise the heads may be boiled off. Cook for 20–30 minutes until all the green parts of the stalks are tender. Drain well, stand in a cool place and serve cold with Chantilly sauce.

TO MAKE THE SAUCE:

Mix ½ pint mayonnaise with 1 tablespoon of lemon juice instead of vinegar. Fold in 2 tablespoons of stiffly beaten cream.

Haricots Verts à la Crème

Put the beans in salted water and boil briskly until three-quarters cooked. Drain and dry in a cloth. Toss the beans in butter for a few seconds, then cover with thick fresh cream. Now simmer until the butter and cream sauce has been reduced to half its original volume. Season to taste and serve.

Asperges Vinaigrette

Put the asparagus in a well-filled saucepan of salted water and boil until tender. Drain, dry carefully with a cloth, then chill. Serve with vinaigrette sauce

TO MAKE THE SAUCE:
To 3 tablespoons of oil add 1 tablespoon of vinegar and 1 teaspoon each of chopped tarragon, chervil, parsley and chives. Thoroughly mix the ingredients and season with salt and freshly ground black pepper. Serve separately in a sauceboat.

Pointes d'Asperges à la Crème

Cut the asparagus heads into even 2-inch lengths, then place them together in bundles. Sections of heads still left on the stalks should be cut into pieces about the size of peas. Wash, then plunge into boiling salted water and cook quickly to keep green. Thoroughly drain and let the moisture evaporate by tossing over heat. Cohere the pea-sized pieces with cream away from the fire, and dish them in a timbale with the bundles on top.

Petits Pois Normands

Cut 5 oz of streaky bacon rashers into thin strips. Peel and finely chop 1 medium onion. Put the bacon strips in a pan with a little clarified butter and heat gently for about a minute. Then add the onion and continue cooking until it is soft and golden brown. Sprinkle just over 1 oz of sieved flour into the pan and stir the mixture with a wooden spoon until the flour and fat combine to form a roux. Gradually stir in cold water until a thin sauce has been made – usually about ⅓ pint will suffice.

Now pour in 1 ½ lb of small shelled peas, season with freshly ground black pepper and add a little salt if required. Cook briskly until the peas are tender.

Pommes Nouvelles

Boil new potatoes in their skins, then peel and serve with melted fresh butter. Sprinkle with a little chopped parsley and season with fine salt and freshly ground white pepper.

Asperges Sauce Mousseline

Plunge the washed asparagus into a large saucepan of boiling salted water – plenty of water is necessary to ensure the temperature does not drop much when the asparagus is added. Cooking time varies according to the quality and the thickness of the asparagus stalks but it should be cooked until still firm. Now carefully remove and drain.

Petits Pois à la Française

(Serves 3-4 people)

2 lb peas
3-4 lettuce leaves, evenly
shredded
bunch parsley or chervil or
    mixture of both
1 dozen small onions
3 ½ oz butter
1 tablespoon plain flour
salt
sugar

After shelling the peas put into a pan with the butter and flour. Place over a very gentle heat and stir rapidly. Add the onions, lettuce leaves, salt and a good pinch of sugar. Distribute the parsley and chervil over the peas, then just cover with cold water. Simmer for about 30 minutes, according to the size of the peas. Serve with a little of the liquid in which they were cooked, which may be slightly thickened with a little beurre manié if preferred.

DINNER FOR TWO

When the Queen and her husband are able to share a palace lunch together, they have what is known in the royal kitchens as an 'all in' lunch. On such occasions the food is laid out on dishes in the Green Tea Room, their private dining room on the first floor of the north wing, and the Queen and Prince Philip serve themselves. The Queen often has a glass of medium-dry sherry and the Prince has his tankard of beer. A duty footman waits outside in the Queen's Corridor for a bell to summon him, should he be required. Except for the periodic private luncheons to meet people, the Queen and her husband seldom entertain at lunch.

If the Queen and her family are dining alone, supper also is generally served in the Green Tea Room. Invariably the meal starts with salad.

Petits Choux Farcis

Small round-headed or Savoy cabbages should be used for this dish.

Parboil them, allow to cool, then take off the stumps. Slightly ease open the leaves and between them place raw or cooked mincemeat, which has been combined with chopped onion and parsley, and highly seasoned. Press the cabbages in close together to restore their shape and wrap them in slices of bacon. Tie neatly with string, then braise them gently for 2 hours with stock and stock fat.

Just before serving, drain the cabbages and remove the string and slices of bacon. Place them on a dish and pour over them a few tablespoons of braising liquor, which has been cleared of all grease and reduced then thickened with half-glaze sauce.

Serve the remaining braising liquor separately with the petits choux.

Laitues Braisés au Jus

Take as many clean, well-hearted lettuces as required and parboil them. Allow them cool and carefully press out the water. Tie them together in twos or threes, according to size, then braise as follows:

First garnish the bottom of a saucepan with blanched pork-rind, sliced onions and carrots, and a faggot. Line the sides with thin slices of bacon. Place the lettuces on top, put the lid on the pan and cook in the oven for about 10 minutes. Remove and just cover with white stock, then cook gently.

When well cooked and tender, cut the lettuces in half, unfold the end of each half, and place on a dish in the form of a crown, alternating the lettuces with heart-shaped croûtons that have been fried in butter.

Haricots Verts Sauté au Beurre

Prepare the beans, then cook carefully for a short amount of time. Ideally they should be a little firm when bitten but not at all hard. When done, season with salt and pepper, them drop in knobs of butter. Sauté the beans until they begin to bind together, then serve at once. Allow about 3 oz of butter to every 1 lb of beans.

Desserts and Cheese

DESSERTS AND SWEETS

*O*ne *of the Queen's preferred ways to conclude a meal is with fruit, particularly grapes. Prince Charles has always had a penchant for lychees, with Peach Melba a close favourite.*

The royal pastry chef has a separate kitchen for making all manner of delicious things for the tea table, including the royal birthday cakes and many varieties of ice cream. It has been a tradition in the royal family to send most of their cakes away to less fortunate children living in orphanages or similar homes, or to hospitals, or homes for the disabled.

When young, Prince Charles was particularly keen on experimenting with recipes, especially ice lollies, and even bought a plastic tray and sticks so he could make them himself – much to the enjoyment of younger brothers Andrew and Edward and sister Anne. Orange and strawberry were the flavours of choice. Ice lollies and jugs of orangeade and lemonade always went down a treat at children's parties in Buckingham Palace.

Like many children, the royal children have always had a great fondness for chocolate, with particular favourites being bars of Kit-Kat. In the days when their great-grandmother, Queen Mary, was still living at Clarence House, Prince Charles and Princess Anne could always be sure of a chocolate feast. Mary herself had a very sweet tooth and always had a big box of chocolates beside her as she worked away at her tapestries. Whenever the little prince and princess came into the room she would tell them to help themselves, and was delighted when they asked her advice on which to choose.

The Queen doesn't eat many sweets and has never encouraged her children to indulge in them, so there were never many about to tempt anyone in the royal suite or the royal nursery. However, especially when younger, the Queen and her sister Margaret had a particular fondness for crisp chocolate-coated peppermint creams, as well as other chocolate and barley sugar sweets that were kept in a big glass jar on a side-table in her drawing room.

DESSERTS

Pêche Melba

ripe peaches
ice cream
blanched almonds
whipped cream

For the sauce:
2 tablespoons water
1 teaspoon cornflower
1 teacup raspberries
(fresh, canned or frozen
raspberries may be used
but if canned no sugar
should be added)
½ teacup redcurrant or
apple jelly

Skin the peaches by plunging in boiling water for 1 minute, then ease off the skin with your fingers. Halve the peaches and remove the stone. Unless the peaches are to be served within minutes of this process, they should not be served raw (when they quickly darken) but should be poached in advance.

Boil 8 oz of sugar in ½ pint of water for 5 minutes, adding a cracked peach stone for extra flavour. Poach the peaches in the sugar syrup until just tender, making sure they do not become mushy; which should take only a few minutes. Chill the peaches well before serving.

TO MAKE THE MELBA SAUCE:
Blend the cornflower with water until smooth and then add raspberries, jelly and sugar, if required, and cook very gently until the mixture thickens. It can be strained through a sieve if desired.

Arrange the fruit and ice cream in individual glasses, placing half a peach, round-side up, on the ice cream, then cover with Melba sauce. Decorate with rosettes of whipped cream and chopped almonds, and serve.

Baba au Rhum

8 oz flour
2 oz sugar
2 eggs
2 oz soft butter
¼ oz powdered yeast
4 tablespoons water
4 tablespoons milk
½ teaspoon vanilla essence
pinch salt
2 tablespoons currants
one tablespoon sultanas

For the syrup:
6 tablespoons rum
½ pint water
½ lb sugar

Heat the milk and water so that it is lukewarm then pour into a bowl and carefully dissolve the yeast in it. Allow to stand for 5 minutes. Into another warmed mixing bowl sift the sugar, flour and a pinch of salt. Then beat the eggs, adding vanilla essence drop by drop. Make a hollow in the centre of the flour and into this, a little at a time, pour first the yeast liquid and then the beaten eggs. While adding the liquid with one hand, use the other (which should be warm) to lightly knead the soft dough that is forming. As soon as it is smoothly blended, place small nuts of the softened butter all over it, then cover lightly with a towel and put in a warm place for it to rise.

A little less than 1 hour should be enough time for the mixture to rise until it has doubled its volume, which is what is required. Now add the currants and sultanas and thoroughly mix in. Fill a large well-buttered ring mould with the dough up to one-third of its height, then cover lightly with a towel and stand in a warm place. When the dough has risen to the rim of the mould put it in a hot oven (425°F/Gas 7) for 10 minutes. Then reduce the heat to 375°F/Gas 5 and continue cooking until the sponge is a rich golden colour. Let it cool sufficiently to turn out.

Now prepare the rum syrup. Stir the sugar and water together in a saucepan, simmer until it begins to thicken, then stir in the rum. Prick the sponge (which should still be warm) all over with a fork, then cover with the hot rum syrup. Continue spooning syrup over the sponge until it has all soaked in.

Just before serving, sprinkle lightly with rum. An optional macédoine of fresh fruits placed around the Rum Baba adds a splendid finishing touch.

Bread and Butter Pudding

3 slices thin bread and butter
2 ozs currants or sultanas
1 egg
½ pint milk
½ oz sugar
nutmeg

Grease a pie dish with butter and place in it a layer of bread and butter (butter side up), which has been cut into neat strips. Sprinkle with fruit and sugar. On top of this place another layer of bread and butter strips, and sprinkle them similarly. Continue until all has been used, remembering not to put fruit on the top layer.

Beat the egg and then add the milk, which should have been heated almost to boiling point. Strain this mixture over the bread, then grate the nutmeg over it. Allow to stand for ½ hour to allow the bread to swell. Now bake in a moderate oven (350°F/Gas 4) for 30 minutes, until the pudding has set firm and is evenly browned on top.

Crèpes Suzettes

(Serves 3–4 people)

5 oz plain flour
2 oz butter
2 oz sugar
½ pint milk
1 egg and 1 yolk
1 orange
1 tablespoon oil or melted butter
2 tablespoons brandy
1 ½ tablespoons curaçao
icing sugar

Sieve the flour into a bowl, make a hollow in the centre and drop in first the whole egg and then the yolk. Next add the melted butter (runny but not hot) or oil. Using a small whisk or spatula blend in the milk and the flour to form a batter with the consistency of thin cream – in no way should it resemble dough. To achieve this consistency, the flour must be mixed in from all sides of the bowl, beating in the milk by degrees, commencing whisking or stirring rapidly at first and decreasing slowly. If the mixture is too thick, add more milk until it is the right consistency.

Peel the orange very carefully ensuring that only the skin comes off and the pith remains on the fruit. Chop the skin very small, meanwhile adding a small amount of the sugar. Soften the butter just enough to make beating easy, then beat it until it is fluffy. Now add the chopped orange skin and the remainder of the sugar and also the curaçao.

Heat a pan until very hot and pour in a little oil, tilting the pan at all angles until its surface is completely filmed with the oil. Pour away any superfluous oil, then pour into the hot pan just sufficient batter to coat its surface very thinly. This should be done delicately so as to avoid anything but the thinnest coating. Now return to the heat until the surface is dry. With a thin-bladed palette ease the edges from the pan, jolting the pan handle sharply with the hand to complete the loosening. Now toss, or turn completely over with the palette or a slice, and cook the reverse side similarly.

On to each cooked crepe spread an even layer of the orange filling and fold into four. Place the filled crepes into a hot buttered dish and dust with icing sugar. When all are ready to serve, warm the brandy, pour it over the crepes and set alight at the moment of serving.

Soufflé Grand Marnier

8 ladyfinger sponges
Grand Marnier
2 tablespoons butter
1 tablespoon flour
powdered sugar
½ cup hot milk
½ teaspoon vanilla extract
5 egg yolks
5 tablespoons sugar
6 egg whites

For the sauce:
½ cup vanilla sauce
¼ cup Grand Marnier
½ cup whipped cream
1 cup milk
1 cup cream
3-inch piece vanilla bean
5 egg yolks
½ cup sugar

Dampen the ladyfinger sponges with Grand Marnier. Melt the butter in a saucepan, add the flour and cook slowly until it begins to turn golden brown. Stir in the hot milk and cook slowly for 5 minutes, stirring or whisking steadily all the time. Add the vanilla extract.

Beat the egg yolks with 4 tablespoons of sugar, then add to the mixture in the pan. Beat the egg whites stiff, adding 1 tablespoon of sugar during the last few minutes. Fold the beaten egg whites carefully and completely into the mixture, raising and folding the mixture over and over.

Pour half of the mixture into a buttered and sugared soufflé dish and cover with the ladyfingers. Fill up with the rest of the mixture and smooth off the top. Bake the soufflé in a moderately hot oven (375°-400°F/Gas 5-6) for 20 minutes, or until well puffed and delicately browned. A few minutes before removing the soufflé from the oven, sprinkle with a little powdered sugar to glaze the top. Serve immediately with the Grand Marnier sauce.

Note: If you would like your soufflé puffed up well above the top of the dish, first tie round a paper collar to give a higher rim, then remove it just before serving the soufflé.

TO MAKE THE GRAND MARNIER SAUCE:

First make the vanilla sauce. Scald the milk, cream and piece of vanilla bean in a double boiler. Beat the egg yolks and sugar well together and combine with the hot milk and cream, stirring or whisking vigorously. Cook over gently boiling water, stirring constantly. When thick enough to coat the spoon, strain the sauce through a fine sieve. Allow to cool, stirring occasionally. If a thicker sauce is preferred add ½ teaspoon of flour to the sugar and yolks.

Now mix the vanilla sauce with the Grand Marnier and fold in the whipped cream. The sauce will keep for 2 days in the refrigerator if required.

Crème Brûlée

6 eggs
1 ½ pints of cream
6 oz brown sugar or 3 oz white sugar
vanilla bean
nutmeg
salt

Whisk or beat the eggs and sugar, adding a pinch of salt and a pinch of freshly grated nutmeg during the process. The final mixture should be light and creamy. Drop a piece of vanilla bean in the cream and scald it. Next stir it gradually into the egg mixture. Pour the mixture into the top of a double boiler over hot water and stir continuously until it coats the spoon, taking care that it does not boil.

Remove the pan from the hot water and put it in a bowl of ice to cool, meanwhile stirring frequently. Pour the custard into heatproof serving cups and coat with brown sugar, so that no custard shows. Brown the top layer of sugar under the grill, making certain it does not burn. Serve cold.

Compote of Fruit

1–1 ½ lb fresh fruit
4–6 oz sugar (according to the acidity of the fruit)
1 level teaspoon arrowroot
wine
cinnamon or nutmeg to flavour
2 gills water

Thoroughly wash and prepare fruit, removing stones and/or peeling as required. Dissolve the sugar in water and boil for about 5 minutes according to the thickness of the syrup desired. Very carefully place the fruit in the syrup and cook gently until tender. Again with extreme care take the fruit out with a spoon.

Blend the arrowroot with 1 tablespoon of cold water and introduce it into the boiling syrup. Cook for 1 minute, stirring all the time. Strain the syrup over the fruit. If you wish to use wine, add if after blending the syrup and arrowroot. If cinnamon or nutmeg is used, they should be mixed in the syrup before it is strained over the fruit.

Cold Plum Pudding

4 oz flour

8 oz raisins

4 oz currants

2 oz bread crumbs

2 oz chopped prunes or dried apricots

4 oz blanched almonds

4 oz shredded suet

4 oz brown sugar

4 oz grated apple

½ pint ale, beer, stout or milk

1 teaspoon mixed spice

1 level teaspoon cinnamon

1 level teaspoon nutmeg

grated rind ½ lemon

1 small grated carrot

4 oz mixed candied peel

grated rind ½ orange

2 eggs

juice ½ lemon

1 tablespoon golden syrup or black treacle

Mix all the ingredients thoroughly together, stirring strongly and well. Leave to stand overnight if possible. Put the mixture into 1 large or 2 smaller basins and cover securely with cloth or paper. Boil or steam for 7-8 hours, then remove and leave to cool. Strip off the wet coverings before doing this. When the puddings are cold put on dry covers and do not remove until required.

AFTER-DINNER RITUALS

The dining room at Balmoral, measuring not much more than 15 foot by 12 foot, has never been enlarged because the Queen's stay is meant to be a real holiday, with only a minimum of guests – rarely more than a dozen sit down to dinner. Life-size portraits of Queen Victoria and Prince Albert look down upon them and voluminous curtains of Balmoral tartan adorn the windows. The diners are always treated to the traditional bagpipe serenade, though again, the smallness of the room precludes more than one piper going in at a time – perhaps another good reason why the dining room hasn't been enlarged! As it is, two or three pipers playing highland music march up and down the corridor outside for about ten minutes. Usually the Pipe Major marches into the dining room to take two or three skirling turns around the table before leaving the diners to their eating and talking.

Following dinner the Queen, Prince Philip and guests retire to an ante-room for coffee and liqueurs before filing into the cinema. The cinema is actually part

of the ballroom but because it is built from local granite it is hardly noticeable from the general construction. When the royal party make their way into the cinema the audience of household staff, gillies and others from the estate stand up to bow or curtsy.

Such courtly manners are general throughout all the royal households. At Sandringham a domestic procedure dating back to the time of Queen Victoria is still observed in the servant's hall. As each of the Queen's housemaids finishes her meal she puts her knife and fork neatly upon her plate and sits quietly with hands on lap. When all have finished, and it is time to leave the table, the Head Housemaid stands up. This is a signal for all the others to do likewise and follow her in stately procession out of the room. Today, however, there is an addition to the ritual: as the procession wends its way past, all the footmen, under-butlers, pages and pantry men beat solemn drum beats on their plates with knife or fork.

Macédoine de Fruits

Mix well in a bowl a variety of fruit in season. This can include pears (quartered or sliced), bananas (peeled and sliced), peaches (sliced), strawberries, raspberries, fresh almonds (blanched), grapes, and so on.

Pour a heavy sugar syrup over the fruit or sprinkle each layer with fine sugar as preferred. The flavour is considerably enhanced by the addition of a few teaspoons of kirsch, maraschino or similar liqueur. Chill well before taking to the table, then serve with fresh double cream.

Eton Mess aux Framboises

Select the finest raspberries, ensure that all the stalks, leaves and blemishes have been removed, then mix well with plenty of thick, rich cream.

Profiteroles au Chocolat

choux pastry
cream

For the sauce:
2 oz plain chocolate
½ oz butter
2–3 tablespoons water

Make choux pastry and put it into a forcing bag fitted with a plain ½-inch nozzle. Pipe it in very small balls on to a baking sheet. Bake the balls for about 25 minutes in a moderately hot oven (400°F/Gas 6) until well risen, crisp and golden brown. Separate and stand on a grid to cool. When cold fill each ball with cream and top with chocolate sauce.

TO MAKE THE CHOCOLATE SAUCE:
Break the chocolate block into small pieces and put them with the butter and water in a small basin standing in hot water in a larger basin. Stir occasionally until the chocolate has melted.

Millefeuilles aux Pommes

Make a flaky pastry, roll it out well and fold it in 3 on itself. Repeat this folding process a further 5 times, by which time the rolled-out pastry should be about ⅓ inch thick. Cut out pieces about 2 inches wide and place them on a baking sheet. Sprinkle well with sugar and bake in a hot oven. When done remove from the oven, stand to cool and trim. Now spread each piece with apple purée and mount one on top of the other, topping with a piece of pastry.

Compote de Mirabelles

Using only the best cooking plums, cut them in half and stone them. Now stew gently in a syrup made with 1 ½ cups of sugar to 2 ½ cups of water. Chill well before serving.

Compote de Pêches

Select only the best ripe peaches and plunge briefly (less than a minute) in boiling water. Now the skins will easily slide off if gently pressed sideways with the fingers. Cut the peaches in half and remove the stones.

Prepare a sugar syrup using 8 oz of sugar and ½ pint of water to which has been added the juice of ½ lemon. Boil for 5 minutes. Now put the peaches in a saucepan, pour the sugar syrup over them, cover with the lid and gently simmer until the peaches are tender. They should be well chilled before serving.

Compote de Poires

Peel, halve and core as many pears as required. Stew them gently until tender in a little water with a lot of sugar added. A little red wine can also be included if preferred. Chill thoroughly and serve.

Bavarois Vanille Sauce Cerises

Put a 1-inch piece of vanilla bean into a cupful of milk and scald. Allow to stand for 10 minutes so that the vanilla flavour is fully absorbed. Lightly beat the yolks of 3 average-sized eggs, gradually add ½ cup of sugar, and continue beating until the mixture is smooth. Now pour the scalded milk slowly into the mixture, stirring constantly.

Cook the mixture over a low heat or in the top of a double boiler in which the water is only simmering. Stir constantly until the liquid coats the back of the spoon. (If cooked over direct heat, remove as soon as it reaches boiling point.)

Take out the vanilla bean, strain the cream into a chilled bowl and add ½ tablespoon of gelatine, which has been softened in 2 tablespoons of cold water, then dissolved over hot water. Stir the cream briskly, allow to cool, then chill until it just begins to thicken sufficiently to retain its shape. Whip 1 cup of double cream until stiff and fold it in. When thick enough to hold its shape, pour the Bavarian vanilla cream into a lightly buttered mould and chill for 3 hours until it is set, or longer if necessary. Turn it out on to a serving dish and serve with sauce cerises.

TO MAKE THE SAUCE:

Rub 1 dozen ripe cherries through a fine sieve and put the pulp into a small copper (or similar) pan. Dilute it with 2 cups of light syrup and bring to the boil. Skim the sauce and remove from the heat when it coats the spoon. Strain or pass through a muslin bag.

A quick and simple method of making this sauce is to dilute cherry jam with hot water, then strain well.

Crème au Caramel

2 whole eggs
2 egg yolks
2 tablespoons sugar
1 pint milk
3 oz castor sugar
3 tablespoons water
squeeze lemon juice (optional)

TO MAKE THE CARAMEL SAUCE:

Put the castor sugar, water and lemon juice into a small, heavy-bottomed saucepan. Place over a low heat and stir until the sugar has dissolved – taking care that the syrup does not boil until all the sugar has melted. Increase the heat and stir occasionally until it is a rich golden colour.

Now remove from the heat and pour into a warmed, buttered soufflé dish or cake tin, which should be continually twisted until the sides and the bottom are evenly coated with the caramel. Beat the eggs and sugar with a fork, heat the milk until almost but not quite boiling and pour on to the beaten eggs. Stir and strain into the soufflé dish or tin – make sure the dish is quite full or the custard may break when turned out.

Next stand it in hot water in a baking tin so that the water reaches halfway up the sides. Cover with a piece of buttered paper or foil and bake in a slow oven (300°F/Gas 2) for 1 hour until quite set. Let the custard get thoroughly cool, then turn it out.

Note: If a very rich custard is desired, use all egg yolks and no whites.

Cherry Tart

2 lb stoned morello cherries
sugar to sweeten
8 oz flour
5 oz butter
1 egg yolk
½ gill melted sharp currant jelly
pinch salt and nutmeg
almond extract

First make a flan pastry. Sift flour and sugar together with a pinch of salt. Using your fingertips, work in the butter until the fat is evenly distributed. Add the egg yolk and, if necessary, add 1 teaspoon of cold water to bind the dough. Chill the dough for 1 hour or more, then roll out.

Line a 9-inch pie dish with the flan pastry and fill with the sweetened cherries. Sprinkle the cherries with nutmeg, salt and almond extract. Bake in a moderate oven (350°F/Gas 4) for about 35 minutes or until the crust is crisply browned and the fruit tender. Stand the tart to cool until lukewarm, then pour over the melted currant jelly. Chill until the glaze is well set.

Rodgrod Med Flode
(Currant Juice with Sago Flour)

1 lb red currants
½ lb raspberries
few bunches blackcurrants
2 oz sago flour

Put all the fruit together in a little water and cook until tender. Strain, then pour just a little of the juice on to the sago flour. Now add all the sago flour to the remainder of the boiling fruit juice and stir over a strong heat for 2 minutes. Remove from the heat and stir continuously until almost cold, then pour into a glass dish. Serve with cream and sugar.

Chocolate Pudding

Using a pre-warmed bowl, work ¼ cup of butter with a wooden spoon until creamy. Add ½ cup of powdered sugar and ¼ teaspoon of vanilla extract (or a few seeds from a split vanilla bean if available). Carry on creaming the mixture until it becomes fluffy. Now work in 6 egg yolks, one by one.

Melt ¼ lb of bitter chocolate in a double saucepan over hot water and add it to the creamed mixture along with 3 tablespoons of flour and 2 tablespoons of arrowroot or cornstarch. Fold in 5 egg whites, which have been beaten stiff.

Rub with butter and dust with flour a ½ quart round or oblong mould, then fill it with the pudding mixture. Set the mould in a pan of hot water and bake the pudding in a moderate oven (350°F/Gas 4) for about 45 minutes. Let the pudding stand for about 15 minutes, then turn it out on to a warmed serving dish. Serve warm with hot chocolate sauce.

Soufflé au Parmesan

Blend 5 tablespoons of sifted flour with 1 cup of boiled milk and season with freshly grated nutmeg, salt and pepper. Place over a brisk heat and stir until boiling. Remove from the heat and add 2 oz of grated Parmesan, 4 teaspoons of butter, 3 egg yolks and 3 beaten egg whites. Mix quickly but steadily and without heating.

Pour the mixture into a buttered soufflé dish, which should be filled no higher than a finger's width from the top. Smooth the surface over and cook in a moderate oven for 20-25 minutes. Serve immediately.

Royal Christmas Pudding

1 lb plums, stoned and
  cut in halves
1 lb small raisins
4 oz candied peel, cut into
  thin slices
4 oz citron, cut into thin slices
1 ½ lb suet, finely shredded
1 lb demerara sugar
1 lb breadcrumbs
1 teaspoonful mixed spice
½ grated nutmeg
1 lb sifted flour
1 lb eggs weighed in their shells
wineglass of brandy
2 teaspoonfuls salt

This recipe has been in the possession of the royal family since the days of George I, with whom it was a great favourite.

Beat the eggs to a light froth, and add to them ½ pint of fresh milk. Thoroughly mix in the other ingredients and allow the mixture to stand for 12 hours in a cool place. Put the pudding mixture into basins or moulds and boil for 8 hours. Three average-sized puddings can be made.

Biscuit Pudding à la Prince Albert

12 oz crumbled Savoy cake
1 pint cream
6 egg yolks
2 egg whites, whipped
lemon rind, rubbed on sugar
4 oz pounded sugar
salt

Boil the cream, then pour on to the crumbled Savoy cake and let it steep for a few minutes. Add the sugar, egg yolks, lemon sugar and a pinch of salt, and lightly mix the whole together. Fold in the egg whites. Pour the preparation into a mould spread with butter, and steam until set.

Pudding à la Française

12 oz chopped marrow
8 oz flour
8 oz apricot jam
4 oz chopped apples
6 oz dried cherries
6 oz candied orange peel and
citron
4 oz sugar
a little grated nutmeg
6 cloves, pounded
1 teaspoon cinnamon powder
zest of rind of 2 oranges rubbed
on sugar
5 eggs
glass brandy
pinch salt
½ pint cream

Put all the ingredients into a large basin, and mix well together. Spread a mould with butter, shake a little flour about the inside, then fill it with the pudding mixture. When done, dish it up with a German custard sauce.

TO MAKE THE SAUCE:
Put four egg yolks into a bain-marie or stew pan, together with 2 oz of pounded sugar, a glass of sherry, orange or lemon peel (rubbed on loaf sugar), and a pinch of salt. Whisk this sharply over a very slow fire, until it assumes the appearance of a light, frothy custard.

Compote of Dried Figs

dried figs
lemon rind, thinly pared
claret
redcurrant jelly
1 bay leaf
castor sugar

Remove the figs from their boxes and put in a pan with the lemon rind and bay leaf. Pour over enough claret just to cover the figs, then add jelly according to taste and sugar. Simmer with the lid on for 20 minutes. Now remove the lid and continue simmering to reduce the liquid until the fruit is only just covered with a rich and sticky juice.

A TASTE FOR CHEESE

Charles is particularly keen on cheese, either to round off a meal or as a snack between meals. Indeed his fondness is such that at times it has had to be strictly controlled – by royal command – when Charles has put on too much weight.

CHEESE

Soufflé au Fromage

3 oz grated cheese (Cheddar
gives a very good texture)
½ oz flour
3 eggs
¼ pint milk
1 oz butter
salt and pepper

Separate the egg yolks from the egg whites, and beat the whites to a still consistency. Then melt the butter and stir in the flour. Slowly pour in the milk and continue stirring while bringing to a gentle boil. When the mixture is a smooth sauce, allow it to cool slightly, then sprinkle in the grated cheese and seasoning, and slide in the egg yolks one after the other, beating well as you do so. Now fold in the beaten egg whites.

Pour the mixture into a previously prepared case and place in the centre of a moderate oven (400°F/Gas 5). Bake for ½ hour, or until well risen and brown. Peel away the paper and serve immediately.

A stiffer soufflé can be obtained by using 1 oz of flour instead of ½ oz.

Céleris au Parmesan

1 head celery
½ pint Mornay sauce
1 handful grated parmesan
melted butter

Cook the celery until tender, then drain well and arrange in a buttered gratin dish. Cover with Mornay sauce and sprinkle with grated Parmesan. Pour about a dessertspoon of melted butter over the celery, then brown in a very hot oven.

Wines

'*The judicious service of wines at the dinner table is essential to the complete success of a well-ordered dinner, for on the order and manner in which this service is conducted will chiefly depend the judgment of the wines put before the guests.*'

Charles Elmé Francatelli, royal cook to Queen Victoria

Francatelli was in many ways responsible for creating many of the instructions and suggestions for the service of wines that became the rule book adopted by many great chefs, as well the royal household, and are still in use today. Francatelli advised:

First, let it be remembered that all possible care should be taken in removing the bottles from their bins, and afterwards also, in handling them for the purpose of drawing the corks, and decanting the wines, not to disturb any deposit that may exist in the bottles, for that deposit, if shaken, destroys not only the brilliancy of the wine, but impairs its flavor and bouquet.

The different kinds of Sherries, Ports, Madeira, and all Spanish and Portuguese wines in general, are the better for having been decanted several hours before being drunk. During winter their aroma is improved by the temperature of the dining room acting upon the volatile properties for an hour or so before dinner time. By paying due attention to this part of the process, all the mellowness, which good wines acquire by age, predominates to the delight of the epicure's grateful palate. The lighter wines, such as Bordeaux Burgundy, and most of the wines of Italy, should be most carefully handled, and decanted an hour only before dinner time. In winter, the decanters should be either dipped in warm water or else placed near the fire, to warm them, for about ten minutes previously to their being used. In summer, use the decanters without warming them, as the genial warmth of the atmosphere will be all-sufficient, not only to prevent chilling

the wines, but to develop their fragrant bouquet. Moreover, let these, and all delicate wines, be brought into the dining room as late as may be consistent with convenience.

And now, as regards the order in which wines should be served during dinner: I would recommend all bon vivants desirous of testing and thoroughly enjoying a variety of wines, to bear in mind that they should be drunk in the following order:

When it happens that oysters preface the dinner, a glass of Chablis or Sauterne is their most proper accompaniment: genuine old Madeira, or East India Sherry, or Amontillado, proves a welcome stomachic after soup of any kind — not excepting turtle — after eating which, as you value your health, avoid all kinds of punch — especially Boman punch. During the service of fish, cause any of the following to be handed round to your guests: Amontillado, Hock, Tisane, Champagne, Pouilly, Meursault, Sauterne, Arbois, vin de Graves, Montrachet, Château Grillet, Barsac, and generally all kinds of dry white wines.

With the entrées, any of the following wines may be introduced:

Bordeaux

Saint-Julien

Leoville

Laroze

Haut-Brion

Château-Lafitte

Château-Margaux

Mouton-Lafitte

Latour

Médoc

Saint Emilion

Saint Estephe

Burgundy, etc.

Mâcon

Moulin-à-vent

Thorins

Beaune

Chassagne

Pale and brown Sherries

Amontillado

Bucellas.

Mancinillo

SECOND-COURSE WINES

Red Wines

Pommard

Volnay

Nuits

Richebourg

Clos-de-Vougeot.

Romanée-Conti

Chambertin

Saint Georges

Pouilly

Meursault

Saint Péray

Rhenish wines (red)

Ermitage

Hermitage

Tavel

Roussillon

Chateauneuf-du-Pape

Côtc-rotic

Jurançon

Monte-Fiascone

Monte-Pulciano

Vino di Pasta

White Wines

Vin de Graves

Sauterne

Barsac

Langon

Ai petillant

Carbonnieux

Champagnes

Red Champagnes

Bouzy

Versy

Volnay mousseux

Veuve Cliquot

Champagne

Sillery.

Sparkling Moselle

Dessert Wines

Muscat-Frontignan

Muscat-Lunel

Muscat-Rivesalte

Grenache

Vin de paille

Malaga

Rota

Alicante

Madeira

Malmsey Madeira

Syracuse

Tokay

Constance

Carcavallos

Picoli

Schiras

A question of the highest importance, but into which I may but briefly enter, is to determine to which of all these wines a decided preference should be given, both with regard to taste, and also in respect to their influence on the health of different temperaments. It is easier to settle the latter part of the question than the former, inasmuch as it is difficult, not to say impossible, to lay down rules for the guidance of the palate. Thus there are some who delight in the perfumed yet austere bouquet of Bordeaux, while others prefer the delicate fragrance of Champagne; some give the palm to the generous and mirth-inspiring powers of Burgundy; while the million deem that Madeira (when genuine), Port, and Sherry, from what are termed their generous natures, ignoring the plentiful admixture of alcohol, are the only wines worthy of notice. All these tastes are no doubt founded on good and sufficient reasons, and may prove safe indicators for the preservation of health: for instance, a person of sanguine temperament feels a necessity for a light sapid wine, such as genuine Champagnes and Rhenish wines; while the phlegmatic seek those of a more spirituous, generous nature – Burgundy, Port, Madeira, or Sherry. Those who are a prey to spleen lowness of spirits (melancholy) are prone to select, as a sure and pleasant remedy for their frightful ailments, the wines of Italy, Spain, Portugal, Roussillon, and Burgundy. The bilious, who generally are blessed with a good appetite, provided always that they do not smoke, require a generous wine, which, while capable of acting both as an astringent and a dissolvent of the bile, is of facile digestion; such are the properties of all first-class Bordeaux wines. Bordeaux is said to be a cold wine; this false notion arises out of mere prejudice – nothing can be more contrary to truth: this health-restoring wine, as I have already stated, is of easy digestion, and possesses, moreover, the advantage of being very considerably less inebriating than any other first-class wine. In short, Burgundy is exciting, Champagne is captious, Roussillon restorative, and Bordeaux stomachic.

It now remains to show the order in which the several sorts of wines, enumerated above, should be served at table. Custom and fashion have ever had more to do with this practice than any real consideration for health or taste.

It is generally admitted by real gourmets that red wines should precede the introduction of white wines – those recommended as proper accompaniments to oysters and fish excepted. The custom most in vogue at the best tables in London and Paris is, to commence by introducing, simultaneously with the entrées, any of the following Burgundy wines: Avallon, Coulanges, Tonnerre, Vermanton, Irancy, Mercurey, Chassagne, and, generally, all those wines known under the specific names of Mâcon and Auxerre: these may be varied or replaced by other wines, denominated Saint Denis, Saint Ay, and Beaugency: these again lead to the further libations of Beaune, Pommard, Volnay, Richebourg, Chambertin, Saint Georges, Romance. With the second course, roasts and dressed vegetables, and savoury entremets, honour your guests by graciously ushering to their notice sparkling Champagne and Moselle, the deliciously perfumed Cumieres, the brilliant Sillery, the glorious Hermitage, Côte-rotie, and Château Grillet.

With the service of the entremets de douceur – or, as we have it, the sweets – let iced-creaming, sparkling champagne or Moselle be handed round; but far superior to them I would recommend a trial of Ai petillant, Arbois, Condrieux, Rivesaltes, Malaga, Frontignan, Grenache, Malmsey, Madeira, and East Indian Sherry.

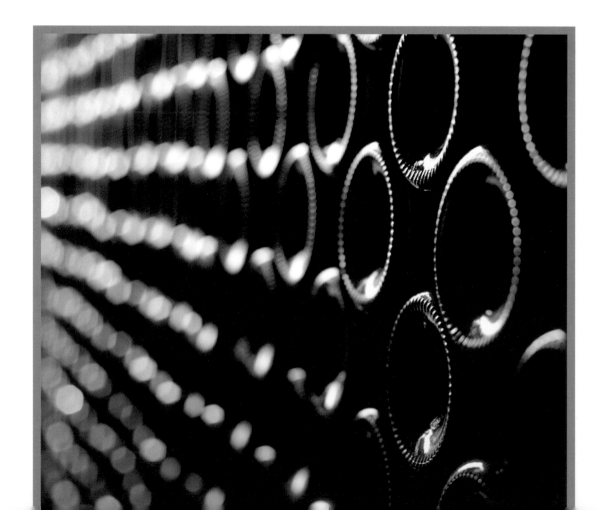

Those Were the Days...

The state occasions during the early reign of Queen Victoria were some of the grandest and most extravagant culinary annual events. The following menus are taken from state banquets held during the last fortnight of August 1841.

THE STOP & GO STATE BANQUETS

In terms of true, almost military-like precision, it would be difficult to improve on a state banquet at Buckingham Palace. For such a great occasion a method had to be devised to organize the efficient serving of food, and a system employing coloured 'stop and go' lights was introduced to ensure that the pages and footmen waiting at table come and go at exactly the right moment.

Printed instructions issued to the staff before a state banquet contain such instructions as:

- The Yeoman of Plate will receive an order from the Page of Chambers when dinner is ready to commence. All staff not detailed for other work must be in their positions by 8.00pm.

- Look to the Palace Steward for signals. An amber light will go on to signal all staff to get into position and ready to handle the plates, and then a green light will flash to commence. All serving staff must commence together.

- Under-butlers will only deal with service, and are responsible for taking everything into and out of the dining room for each course. They will also assist in the main course, serving the vegetable dishes.

The waiting staff are specially warned to keep to the particular service specified for them and in no circumstances must they try and help out if they see things are not running smoothly in other parts of the banqueting hall. Should waiters about to enter see a red light flash from beside the throne, they must stop and wait for the green light.

Wine pages are instructed to leave the banqueting room immediately after they have handed the port round (which must circulate clockwise), then they must go to the State Dining Room to serve liqueurs. Coffee is afterwards served in several of the beautiful drawing rooms in the state apartments.

At state banquets the Queen and her principal guests sit in the centre of the curve of a horseshoe-shaped table. The Steward operating the stop-go lights stands just behind the Queen and slightly to one side, so that he is directly opposite the door through which the footmen, pages and under-butlers enter and leave the room. On such occasions all the men waiting at table wear scarlet frock coats and white satin knee breeches, with white silk stockings and gloves. Until fairly recently, they also had to wear powdered white wigs.

The Steward flashes a light for a course

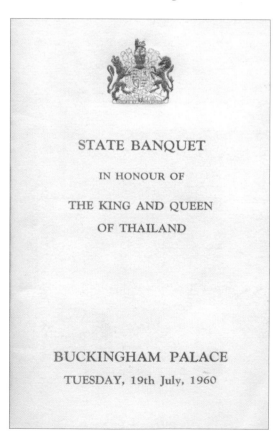

STATE BANQUET

IN HONOUR OF

**THE KING AND QUEEN
OF THAILAND**

BUCKINGHAM PALACE

TUESDAY, 19th July, 1960

to be cleared away only when he has ascertained that the Queen and all her guests have finished and are ready for the next course – at which point the page in charge of the course sends his men surging in with it.

Since these occasions are generally attended by some 150 guests, who are served both a buffet supper and an after-the-ball palace breakfast (shortly after 1 a.m), washing up can be quite a business. Throughout the banquet the gold plate is handled only by the Gold Room staff and the silver plate only by Silver Room staff. Every item taken out of the strongroom in the palace vaults is counted, and then counted again when returned. Such careful attendance of staff would make it seemingly impossible for a souvenir-hunting guest to smuggle out a plate, though no doubt – like Edwards VII's brave American guest (see Chapter 4) – there are those who have tried. The gold is taken into a special washroom, where it is washed in warm water and then polished.

The Queen's Household

Mary, Duchess of Devonshire (Mistress of the Robes)

The Countess of Euston (Lady of the Bedchamber)

The Lady Rose Baring (Woman of the Bedchamber)

The Earl of Scarbrough (Lord Chamberlain) and the Countess of Scarbrough

The Duchess of Hamilton and Brandon

Lieutenant-General the Lord Freyberg, V.C. (Deputy Constable and Lieutenant-Governor of Windsor Castle) and the Lady Freyberg

The Earl St. Aldwyn (The Captain, Gentlemen-at-Arms) and the Countess St. Aldwyn

The Earl of Onslow (The Captain, Yeomen of the Guard) and the Countess of Onslow

Lieutenant-Colonel the Right Hon. Sir Michael Adeane (Private Secretary) and Lady Adeane

Brigadier the Lord Tryon (Keeper of the Privy Purse) and the Lady Tryon

Major M. V. Milbank (Master of the Household)

Lieutenant-Colonel Sir Terence Nugent (Comptroller, Lord Chamberlain's Office)

Brigadier Walter Sale (Crown Equerry)

Commander Philip Row, R.N. (Deputy Treasurer) and Mrs. Row

Major-General Sir Guy Salisbury-Jones (Marshal of the Diplomatic Corps)

Lieutenant-Colonel the Hon. Martin Charteris (Assistant Private Secretary) and the Hon. Mrs. Charteris

Brigadier Sir Norman Gwatkin (Assistant Comptroller, Lord Chamberlain's Office)

The Lord Plunket (Equerry in Waiting)

Lieutenant-Commander Peter Campbell, R.N. (Equerry)

Rear-Admiral Sir Arthur Bromley, Bt. (Gentleman Usher)

The Duke of Edinburgh's Household

Lieutenant-General Sir Frederick Browning (Treasurer)

Queen Elizabeth The Queen Mother's Household

The Dowager Duchess of Northumberland (Mistress of the Robes)

Lieutenant-Colonel the Earl of Airlie (Lord Chamberlain) and the Countess of Airlie

The Hon. Iris Peake (Lady in Waiting to The Princess Margaret)

The Duchess of Kent's Household

Mr. Philip Hay (Comptroller and Private Secretary)

HER MAJESTY'S DINNER
25TH JANUARY 1841

Potages:

A la tête de veau en tortue

De quenelles de volaille au consommé

Poissons:

Le saumon à la sauce homard

Les soles frites à la sauce hollandaise

Relevés:

Le filet de boeuf, pique braise aux pommes de terre

Le chapon à la godard

Entrées:

Le bord de pommes de terre, garni de palais de boeuf

La chartreuse de perdrix aux choux

Les cotelettes d'agneau panées

La blanquette de volaille à l'ecarlate

Les lapereaux, sautés aux fines herbes

Les petits pâtés aux huitres

Rots:

Les poulets

Les faisans

Relevés:

Le pudding à l'orange
Les omelettes soufflées

Entremets:

Les pommes de terre à la Strasbourgeoise
Les epinards au jus
La gelée de marasquin
Les petites talmouses
Les feuillantines de pommes
La crème aux amandes pralinées

Buffet:

Roast beef and mutton
Boiled round of beef

HER MAJESTY'S DINNER
30TH JUNE 1841

4 Hors d'oeuvres:

Les petits pâtés de homards

Potages:

Printannier
A la reine
A la tortue

Poissons:

Les truites à la sauce Genèvoise
Le Turbot à la sauce homardLes filets de merlans frits
Les whitebait frits

4 Relevés:

Les oulardes truffées à la sauce Périgueux
Le jambon glacé garni de fèves de marais
La selle d'agneau farcie à la royale
Le filet de boeuf pique à la Napolitaine

16 Entrées:

2 Les nageoires de tortue sauce au vin de Madère
2 Les filets de poulets à l'écarlate aux concombres

2 Les cotelettes de mouton braisées à la purée d'artichauds
2 Les aiguillettes de canetons aux pois verts
2 Les riz de veaux piqués glacés à la Toulouse
2 Les cotelettes de pigeons panées à l'allemande
2 Les chartreuse de tendons d'agneau à l'essence
2 Les timbales de macaroni à la mazarine

Side Board:

Haunch of venison
Roast beef
Roast mutton
Vegetables

Second Service

6 Rots:

2 levrauts
2 de poulets
2 de cailles

6 Relevés:

2 Les puddings à la Nesselrode
2 Les puddings de cabinet
2 Les soufflés à la fécule de pommes de terre

2 Flancs :

Le pavilion mauresque
La tente militaire

4 Contre-Flancs :

Le nougat aux amandes.
Le biscuit de savoie à la vanilleLa sultane Parisienne
Le croque-en-bouche historique

16 Entremets :

Les truffes au vin de Champagne
Les artichauts à la Lyonnaise
Le buisson de prawns sur socle
L'anguilles en volute au beurre de Montpellier
Les tartelettes de framboisesLa gelée de groseilles garnie de pêche
Les genoises aux fruits transparents
Les petits pois à la Française
Les haricots verts à la poulette
L'aspic de blancs de volaille à la Bellevue
La salade de legumes a l'italienne
La macédoine de fruits
Le bavaroix de chocolat panache
La crème aux amandes pralinées
Les petits pains à la Parisienne
Les gateaux de Pithiviers

HER MAJESTY'S DINNER
15ᵀᴴ AUGUST 1841

Potages :

A la croute gratinée à la Sévigné
A la purée de gelinottesA la crème de riz garni de
quenelles au beurre d'écrivisses

Poissons :

Le brochet garni d'une matelotte d'anguilles.
Les filets de merlans frits
Les truites sauce a la pluche

Relevés :

Les poulardes au macaroni
Le gigot de mouton de sept heuresLe jambon aux petits pois
Les queux de boeufs à la jardinière

Entrées :

Les cotelettes d'agneau sautées aux concombres
Les filets de lapereaux panés a l'allemande
Les cervelles de veau marinées frites sauce tomates
Les escalopes de gelinottes aux truffes
Les pieds de veau aux petits pois
Les fricassée de poulets dans un bord de riz

Rots:

Les dindonneaux
Les canetons

Relevés:

Le pudding de sagou sauce au fruit
Le soufflé au citronLes beignets de pêches

Flancs:

Le schapska polonais
Le melon en nougat

Entremets:

Le bastion d'anguilles au beurre de Montpellier
Le buisson de truffes au vin de Champagne
Les concombres à la poulette
Les haricots verts sautés au beurre
La gelée de Malaga
La macédoine de fruit
Les tartelettes de prunes de Reine Claude
Les petits gateaux feuilletés à l'abricot
Le pain de gibier à la gelée
La salade à la russe
Les pommes de terre a la maître d'hôtel
La macédoine de légumes
Le bavaroix aux framboises
La crème au café mocha
Les pains de la mecque à la Chantilly
Les dauphines à la fleur d'orange

Side Board:

Roast beef

Roast mutton

Roast venison

Riz au consommé

Emincé de poulet aux Oeufs poches

Haricots verts

Currant tart

HER MAJESTY'S DINNER
16TH AUGUST 1841

Potages:

A la tortue
A la cressy
A la royale

Poissons:

Le St Pierre à la sauce homard
Les filets de soles à la ravigotteLes gougeons frits sauce hollandaise
Le saumon sauce aux capres

Relevés:

La pièce de boeuf à la flamande
Les poulardes et langues aux choux-fleursLe pâté-chaud de pigeons a l'anelaise
La noix de veau en bedeau

Entrées:

Les cotelettes de mouton à la purée d'artichauts
Les boudins de lapereaux à la Richelieu
Les pieds d'agneau en canelons farcis à l'italienne
Les filets de poulardes à la régence
Les tendons de veau glacés à la macédoine
Les petites timbales de nouilles à la purée de gelinottes

Rots:

Les chapons
L'oie
Les combattants

Relevés:

Le pudding de riz
Le baba au rhum
Les beignets au Parmesan

Flams:

La cascade ornée de sucre filé
La chaumière rustique

Entremets:

La darne d'esturgeon au beurre de Montpellier
Le buisson d'ecrivisses
Les petits pois à la Française
Les haricots verts à la maître d'hôtel
La gelée au vin de Champagne
La crème au caramel
Les petits gateaux de crème à l'anglaise
La tourte de pêches
L'aspic de volaille à la Belle-vue
Les ponds d'artichauts à la provençale
Les concombres farcis a l'essence
Les choux-fleurs à la sauce
Le bavaroix de fraises
La gelée de pêches
Les tartelettes de cerises
Le gateau de Pithiviers

Side Board:

Roast beef
Hashed venison
Roast mutton
Riz au consommé
Plum and Yorkshire puddings

HER MAJESTY'S DINNER
20TH AUGUST 1841

Potages:

A la tortue

A la faubonne

A la xavier

Poissons:

Le saumon ciselé sauce homar

Les eglefins sauce aux oeufs

Les merlans frits sauce hollandaise

Relevés:

Le jambon de Westphalie aux haricots verts

La pièce de boeuf à la mazarine

Les poulardes à la Belle-vue sauce suprème

L'oie braisée garnie de racines

Entrées:

Les cotelettes de mouton à la purée de pommes de terre

Les ballottines de volailles à la jardinière

Les fricandeaux glacés à la purée de pois

Les ailerons de poulets panés à la villeroi

Les petites croustades à la purée de gelinottes

Les boudins à la reine

Rots:

Gelinottes

Poulets

Wheatears

Releves:

Les beignets soufflés au citron
Le pudding roule à l'allemandeLe pudding bavaroix

Flancs:

Les canards à la Chantilly
La condole vénitienne

Entremets:

Les anguilles en bastion
Les écrevisses au vin
Les artichauts à la provençale
La macédoine de légumes
La gelée de pêches
La charlotte russe
Les tartelettes de cerises à la crème
Les génoises aux confitures
L'aspic de galantine
Les truffes à la serviette
Les petits pois à l'anglaise
Les haricots verts à la maître d'hôtel
Le bavaroix de framboises
Les petits puits d'amour
Les dauphines aux pistaches

Side Board:

Roast beef
Roast mutton
Haunch of venison Riz au consommé
Marrow on toast

HER MAJESTY'S DINNER
END OF AUGUST 1841

Potages:

De Quenelles au Consommé

A la Garbure aux Laitues

A la purée de Gelinottes

Poissons:

Les brochets farcis au four

Les anguilles à la tartareLe turbot sauce homard

Relevés:

Les carrés de venaison en chevaux-de-frize

Le pâté de pigeons à l'anglaise

Entrées:

Les petits poulets aux choux-fleurs

Les poitrine d'agneau à la dauphine

Les blanquettes de volaille aux concombres

Les boudins de volaille à la Sefton

Les chartreuses de tendons de veau

Les petits pâtés aux huitres

Rots:

Wheatears

Les levrauts

Les dindonneaux

Relevés:

Les gaufres à la flamande
Le pudding soufflé au citron

Entremets:

La darne saumon à la remoulade
La salade à la russe
Le macaroni à l'italienne
Les oeufs à l'aurore
Les artichauts à la Lyonnaise
Les haricots verts à la poulette
La gelée de citron garnie de prunes vertes
Le bavaroix à la canelle
Les feuillantines aux pommes
Le flan de fruit
Les petits biscuits aux amandes
Les pêches au riz à la conde

Side Board:

Roast beef
Roast mutton
Hashed venison
Riz au consommé
Greengage tart
Petits pots de volaille

Menus for Every Month of the Year

*T*he following are a selection of menus that have been previously served on royal occasions. Each month has its own distinctive culinary character.

JANUARY

Dinner for 6 persons

1 SOUP:
Palestine

1 FISH:
Crimped cod and oyster sauce

2 REMOVES:
Roast griskin of pork with apple sauce
Braised pheasant with cabbages

2 ENTRÉES:

Patties of chicken à la béchamel

Mutton cutlets sautées with purée of potatoes

SECOND COURSE

1 ROAST:

Hare

3 ENTREMETS:

Fried salsifis in batter

Orange jelly

Apricot puffs

Dinner for 6 persons

1 SOUP:

Oxtail clear soup

1 FISH:

Broiled herrings, with mustard sauce

2 REMOVES:

Snipe pudding, à la d'Orsay

Roast saddle of mutton

2 ENTRÉES:

Blanquette of fowl with mushrooms

Scallops of beef à la Napolitaine

SECOND COURSE

1 ROAST:

Pheasant

3 ENTREMETS:

Brussels-sprouts à la crème
Meringues with cream
Pears and rice à la Condé

Dinner for 6 persons

1 SOUP:

Jardinière clear soup

1 FISH:

Whitings au gratin

2 REMOVES:

Roast neck of venison
Braised pheasant with soubise sauce

2 ENTRÉES:

Quenelles of fowl à l'essence
Tendons of veal with a purée of spinach

SECOND COURSE

1 ROAST:

Larks

3 ENTREMETS:

Brown-bread pudding à la Gotha (preserved cherries)
Turnips glacés à l'espagnole.
Apple fritters

FEBRUARY

Dinner for 8 persons

1 SOUP:
Cream of barley à la reine

2 FISH:
Matelote of eels
Crimped cod broiled with Dutch sauce

2 REMOVES:
Pheasants à la financière
Braised roll of beef à la flamande
Noukles with Parmesan

2 ENTRÉES:
Scallops of fowls a l'écalarte
Lamb cutlets breadcrumbed with a purée of celery

SECOND COURSE

2 ROASTS:
Teal
Macaroni à l'italienne

1 REMOVE:
Rice soufflée

4 ENTREMETS:
Canapés of anchovies
Seakale à la béchamel
Tourte of pears à la Cobourg
Burnt cream au caramel

Dinner for 8 persons

SOUPS
Soup à la Desclignac

2 FISH:
Crimped haddocks, Dutch sauce
Fillets of brill à la maréchale

2 REMOVES:
Roast haunch of mutton
Braised goose à la jardinière

Lobster patties

2 ENTRÉES:
Chickens à la Marengo
Salmis of snipes à la Talleyrand

SECOND COURSE

2 ROASTS:
Black game
Salad à la russe

1 REMOVE:

Nouilles cake à l'allemande

4 ENTREMETS:

Celery à la Villeroi

Profiteroles à la crème

Poached eggs on anchovy toast

Apricot cheese à la Chantilly

Dinner for 8 persons

1 SOUP:

Hare soup à la chasseur

2 FISH:

Turbot, lobster sauce

Broiled whitings, capers' sauce

2 REMOVES:

Capon and rice

Braised leg of mutton à la soubise

Patties à la mazarin

2 ENTRÉES:

Grenadins of veal larded, garnished with a nivernaise

Fillets of pheasants à la maréchale

SECOND COURSE

2 ROASTS:
Potato chips
Ptarmigans

1 REMOVE:
Apple pudding

4 ENTREMETS:
Braised celery, garnished with croustades of marrow
Orange jelly, à l'anglaise
Bread-and-butter pastry
Scalloped oysters

MARCH

Dinner for 6 persons

1 SOUP:

Brown purée of turnips

1 FISH:

Soles à la Colbert

2 REMOVES:

Boiled fowl, with broccoli

Roast leg of lamb

2 ENTRÉES:

Mutton cutlets sautées with a purée of potatoes

Vol-au-vent of godiveau à la financiére

SECOND COURSE

Roast widgeon

3 ENTREMETS:

Eggs brouillés with asparagus-peas

Tapioca pudding, custard sauce

German tourte of apples

Dinner for 6 persons

1 SOUP:

Paysanne

1 FISH:

Crimped skate fried, with capers' sauce

2 REMOVES:

Braised neck of mutton à l'irlandaise

Lark pudding à la chipolata

2 ENTRÉES:

Timbale of raviolis à la romaine

Chickens à l'allemande

SECOND COURSE

Roast duckling

3 ENTREMETS:

Scalloped muscles

Cranberry tart

Lemon and cinnamon cream

Dinner for 6 persons

1 SOUP:

Cream of rice à la Victoria

1 FISH:

Fried eels à la tartare

2 REMOVES:

Lamb's head à la galimafrée

Fowl à la dauphine

2 ENTRÉES:

Beefsteaks à la Française

Braised duck à la nirvernaise

SECOND COURSE

1 ROAST:

Pigeons

3 ENTREMETS:

Jerusalem artichokes à l'espagnole

Cherry bread à la Gotha

Puff-paste tartlets of raspberry-jam

APRIL

Dinner for 12 persons

2 SOUPS:
Spring soup
Bisque of crayfish à la Malmesbury

2 FISH:
Crimped salmon with parsley and butter sauce
Perch à la Stanley

2 REMOVES:
Calf's head à la beauveau
Poulards and tongue à la macédoine.

4 ENTRÉES:
Lambs cutlets à la duchesse
Fillets of fowls with asparagus-peas, suprème sauce
Boudins of lobster à la carnidal
Fritot of spring chickens with poivrade sauce

SECOND COURSE

2 ROASTS
Ducklings
Guinea fowls, larded

2 REMOVES:
Steamed soufflée
Compiegne cake

6 ENTREMETS:
Broccoli with white sauce
Spinach in small croustades
Loaves à la Parisienne
Gooseberry cream
Flan of pears and rice à la Condé
Cherry jelly

Dinner for 12 persons

2 SOUPS:
Quenelles of fowl in consommé
Purée of young carrots à la faubonne

2 FISH:
Spey trout, Dutch sauce
Fillets of soles à la Bagration

2 REMOVES:
Roast forequarter of lamb
Chickens à la printanière

4 ENTRÉES:
Veal cutlets à la dreux
Scallops of fowls with cucumbers
Fillets of mutton larded, with tomato sauce
Boudins of rabbit à la Pompadour

SECOND COURSE

2 ROASTS:
Pigeons
Turkey poults

2 REMOVES:

Ramequins à la Sefton

Biscuits glacés, in cases

6 ENTREMETS:

Seakale with white sauce

Mushrooms au gratin

Vol-au-vent of macédoine

Gooseberry tartlets

Pudding à la viennoise

Marbled cream

Dinner for 16 persons

2 SOUPS:

Macaroni clear soup

Purée of spinach à la Condé

2 FISH:

Crimped turbot, lobster sauce

Matelote of eels à la bordelaise

2 REMOVES:

Braised saddle of lamb à la jardinière

Poulards à l'estragon

Shrimp patties, to be handed round

6 ENTRÉES:

Mutton cutlets with new potatoes

Sweetbreads larded à la Parisienne

Fillets of pigeons à la dauphine with French beans

Fillets of ducklings à la bigarade

Quenelles of fowl à la Périgueux

Quails au gratin with financière sauce

SECOND COURSE

2 ROASTS:

Peahen larded

Green goose

2 REMOVES:

Brioche with cheese

Chocolate soufflé

8 ENTREMETS:

Asparagus with white sauce

French beans à la Poulette

Macédoine jelly

Pudding à la Prince de Galles

Vanilla cream

Apricot tartlets

Porcupine of apples meringue

Lobster salad

MAY

Dinner for 8 persons

1 SOUP:
Bisque of prawns

2 FISH:
Trout, Dutch sauce
Whitebait

2 REMOVES:
Roast poularde à l'italienne
Boiled leg of lamb and spinach

Patties of ox-piths au jus

2 ENTRÉES:
Pigeon cudets à la dauphine
Scallops of fillets of beef à la Claremont

SECOND COURSE

2 ROASTS:
Plovers' eggs plain
Green goose

1 REMOVE:
Apricot soufflé

4 ENTREMETS:
Green peas plain
Burnt cream au caramel
New potatoes au gratin
Strawberry tartlets

Dinner for 8 persons

1 SOUP:
Purée of fowls à la Célestine

2 FISH:
Crimped soles, Dutch sauce
Red mullets in cases with fine herbs

2 REMOVES:
Chickens à la reine
Ribs of beef à la mode
Lobster patties

2 ENTRÉES:
Boudins of rabbit à la Richelieu.
Mutton cutlets with stewed peas

SECOND COURSE

2 ROASTS:
Crayfish plain
Ducklings

1 REMOVE:
Pancakes with apricot

4 ENTREMETS:
New potatoes à la crème
Macaroni au gratin
D'artois of strawberry jam
Maraschino jelly

Dinner for 8 persons

1 SOUP:
Desclignac, with asparagus points

2 FISH:
Small turbot, lobster sauce
Epigramme of fillets of trout

2 REMOVES:
Braised green goose à la flamande
Roast quarter of lamb à la maître d'hôtel

Soft roes of mackerel fried in batter, Gascony sauce

2 ENTRÉES:
Chickens à la florentine
Tendons of veal with a macédoine of vegetables

SECOND COURSE

2 ROASTS:
Canapés of anchovies
Turkey poult, larded

1 REMOVE:
Flemish gaufres

4 ENTREMETS:
Seakale à la béchamel
New potatoes à la maître d'hôtel
Orange-flower cream
Raspberry tartlets

JUNE

Dinner for 6 persons

1 SOUP:

Green-pea à la Condé

1 FISH:

Baked whitings with fine herbs

2 REMOVES:

Chicken pie à l'anglaise

Breast of veal and stewed peas

2 ENTRÉES:

Mutton cutlets à la Milanaise

Rabbit curry in a border of rice

SECOND COURSE

1 ROAST:

Pigeons

3 ENTREMETS:

Stewed peas à la Française

Bavarian strawberry cream

Puff-paste royals

Dinner for 6 persons

1 SOUP:
Clear rice

1 FISH:
Fillets of mackerel à la maître d'hôtel

2 REMOVES:
Poulard à l'Ivoire
Braised neck of mutton à l'allemande

2 ENTRÉES:
Minced beef à la polonaise
Tourte of godiveau à la financière

SECOND COURSE

1 ROAST:
Duckling

ENTREMETS
Cauliflowers with white sauce
Dutches loaves with apricot jam
Timbale of ground rice

Dinner for 6 persons

1 SOUP:

Bonne-femme

1 FISH:

Broiled trout, Dutch sauce

2 REMOVES:

Roast leg of Welsh mutton

Noix of veal à la crème

2 ENTRÉES:

Mince of fowl with poached eggs

Fillets of beef in their glaze, garnished with stewed peas

SECOND COURSE

1 ROAST

Fowl

3 ENTREMETS:

Asparagus with sauce

Apricot nougat

Maraschino jelly with strawberries

JULY

Dinner for 12 persons

2 SOUPS:
Vermicelli clear soup
Brown purée of turnips à la Condé

2 FISH:
Fried flounders
Char à la Génoise

Noukles with Parmesan

2 REMOVES:
Fillet of beef, chevreuil sauce
Chickens and tongue à la printanière

4 ENTRÉES:
Cutlets of breasts of lamb à la villeroi with French beans
Compote of pigeons with peas
Quenelles of lobster à la vert-pré
Pâté-chaud of young rabbits with fine herbs

SECOND COURSE

2 ROASTS:
Peahen larded
Ducklings

2 REMOVES:
Parmesan fritters
Polish Baba

4 ENTREMETS:

Young broad beans à la poulette

Aspic of prawns à la russe

Peaches with rice à la Condé

Puff-paste plats

Dinner for 12 persons

2 SOUPS:

Consommé soup à la Xavier

Green-pea soup à la Fabert

2 FISH:

Whitebait

Salmon à l'écossaise

Shrimp patties

2 REMOVES:

Poulard à la Godard

Necks of lamb larded, à la macédoine

4 ENTRÉES:

Mutton cutlets bread crumbed and broiled with shallot gravy

Tendons of veal on a border of vegetables, garnished with peas

Vol-au-vent à la financière

Blanquette of fowls à l'écarlate

SECOND COURSE

2 ROASTS:

Guinea-fowls

Quails

2 REMOVES:

Omelette soufflée

Coburg cake

4 ENTREMETS:

Cucumbers farcis à l'essence

Stewed peas à la Française

Tourte of currants and raspberries

Blancmange

Dinner for 14 persons

2 SOUPS:

Brunoise printanière

Bisque of crayfish à l'ancienne

2 FISH:

John-Dory, lobster sauce

Trout à la chevalière

Croquettes of ox palattes

2 REMOVES:

Braised ham with broad beans

Poulards à la Périgord

4 ENTRÉES:

Mutton cutlets à la Pompadour, garnished with a macédoine

Lambs' sweetbreads larded, with purée of artichokes

Scallops of quails with fumet sauce and truffles, garnished with
small croustades of purée

Fillets of fowls à la Bellevue with suprême and cucumbers

SECOND COURSE

2 ROASTS:
Spring chickens
Ducklings

2 REMOVES:
Dauphine fritters
Vanilla soufflés in cases

4 ENTREMETS:
French beans à la maître d'hôtel
Aspic of plovers' eggs and prawns
Strawberry jelly
Profiteroles à la vanille

AUGUST

Dinner for 12 persons

2 SOUPS:

Desclignac soup

Purée of carrots à la Crécy

2 FISH:

Soles à la Colbert

Red mullets à l'italienne

Anchovy patties à la mazarin

2 REMOVES:

Capon à la milanaise

Braised necks of mutton larded, a l'allemande

4 ENTRÉES:

Blanquette of lambs' sweetbreads à la paysanne

Salmis of grouse à la bordelaise

Tourte of whitings à la dauphine

Mutton cutlets à la provençale

SECOND COURSE

2 ROASTS:

Chickens

Wheatears

2 REMOVES:

Fondu of Parmesan

Viennoise pudding

4 ENTREMETS:

Vegetable marrow à la crème

Codling cheese à la Chantilly

Potatoes à la hollandaise

Génoise cakes with pistachios

Dinner for 12 persons

2 SOUPS:

Macaroni in consommé

Purée of spinach à la beauveau

2 FISH:

Water-souchet of perch

Slices of salmon broiled, with capers' sauce

Patties au jus

2 REMOVES:

Roast saddle of mutton

Grouse pie à l'écossaise

4 ENTRÉES:

Fricassée of chickens à la financière

Members of ducks à la nivernaise

Epigramme of lamb with a purée of potatoes

Fillets of leverets larded, with poivrade sauce

SECOND COURSE

2 ROASTS:

Guinea fowls

Ruffs and Reeves

2 REMOVES:

Omelette with apricot

Cherry bread

4 ENTREMETS:

French beans à la poulette

Artichokes with white sauce

Flan of peaches

Coffee cream

Dinner for 12 persons

2 SOUPS:

Consommé of fowl with quenelles

Hodge-Podge à l'écossaise

2 FISH:

Fried whitings, Dutch sauce

Charr à la Parisienne

Oyster patties

2 REMOVES:

Roast haunch of venison

Capon au gros-sel

4 ENTRÉES:

Chartreuse à la cardinal

Fricandeau à la jardinière

Members of chickens à la maréchale

Mutton cutlets with purée of turnips

SECOND COURSE

2 ROASTS:

Peahen larded

Grouse

2 REMOVES:

Custard fritters

Apple pudding with apricot jam

4 ENTREMETS:

Vegetable marrow à l'espagnole

Spinach with cream

Blancmange

Florentines

SEPTEMBER

Dinner for 16 persons

2 SOUPS:
Vermicelli à la royale
Oxtail soup

2 FISH:
Cod à la béchamel
Broiled haddocks, Dutch sauce

2 REMOVES:
Fowls and tongue with cauliflowers
Haunch of red deer à la Kinnaird

6 ENTRÉES:
Fillets of grouse, breadcrumbed à la maître d'hôtel
Croustade garnished with lambs' brains with matelote sauce
Mutton patties à la Windsor
Tourte of scallops of lobsters à la cardinal
Minced beef à la polonaise
Chickens sautés à la Lyonnaise

SECOND COURSE

2 ROASTS:
Black game
Partridges

2 REMOVES:
Sweet omelette
Chestnut pudding

6 ENTREMETS:

Tomates au gratin

Fried artichokes

Lemon jelly à la russe

Bavarian chocolate cream

D'artois of apple marmalade

Petits-choux with almonds

Dinner for 16 persons

SOUPS:

Purée of endives à la crème

Giblet soup à l'irelandaise

2 FISH:

Eels à la tartare

Salmon with lobster sauce

2 REMOVES:

Veal and ham pie

Braised goose à l'estouffade

6 ENTRÉES:

Ox-piths in small cases, with fine herbs

Partridges à la Périgueux

Croustades à la Milanaise

Quenelles of whitings, with crayfish sauce

Vol-au-vent of lambs' feet à la poulette

Blanquette of fowl with mushrooms

SECOND COURSE

2 ROASTS

Capon

Leveret

2 REMOVES:

Puff-paste ramequins

Tapioca pudding

6 ENTREMETS:

Spinach au jus

Vegetable marrow à la béchamel

Charlotte of apricots

Noyau jelly

Burnt almond cream

Cheese cakes

Dinner for 24 persons, Russian style

3 SOUPS:

Soup à la Colbert

White purée of turnips

Giblet soup

3 FISH:

Fillets of gurnets à l'italienne

Fried soles

Crimped cod with oyster sauce

Patties à la béchamel

3 REMOVES:

Boiled leg of mutton

Black game à la norvégienne

2 roast geese à l'anglaise

6 ENTRÉES:

2 sweetbreads larded, with purée of endives.

2 cutlets of young partridges à la maréchale

2 haricot of venison à la nivernaise

SECOND COURSE

3 ROASTS:

Wheatears

Pigeons

Poulard

3 REMOVES:

Parmesan fritters

Pancakes soufflés

Pudding à la Nesselrode

8 ENTREMETS:

2 French beans sautés with butter

2 pears with rice à la Condé

2 scalloped lobsters au gratin

2 Vol-au-vents of greengages

OCTOBER

Dinner for 12 persons

2 SOUPS:
Julienne soup

Mock turtle soup

2 FISH:
Cod's head, baked

Fillets of soles à la dieppoise

2 REMOVES:
Ham, with spinach

Roast fillet of veal à la macédoine

4 ENTRÉES:
Suprême of fowls à la Talleyrand

Mutton cutlets à l'indienne

Oyster patties à la Sefton

Fillets of woodcocks à l'ancienne

SECOND COURSE

2 ROASTS:
Hare

Pheasants

2 REMOVES:
Brioche with cheese

Soufflé of chocolate

4 ENTREMETS:
Mushrooms à la provençale
Scalloped crayfish
German apple tourte
Pineapple jelly

Dinner for 12 persons

2 SOUPS:
Purée of spinach à la Conti
Soup à la paysanne.

2 FISH:
Fried soles, shrimp sauce
Crimped cod à la Seville

2 REMOVES:
Roast saddle of mutton
Partridge pie à l' Anglaise

4 ENTRÉES:
Fillets of teal à la provençale
Scallops of beef sautés, with oyster sauce
Ballotines of legs of chickens à la financière
Croquettes of sweetbreads à l'allemande

SECOND COURSE

2 ROASTS:
Larks
Grouse

2 REMOVES:

Omelette with Parmesan

Pancakes with apricot

4 ENTREMETS:

Croûtes with mushrooms

Damson cheese à la Chantilly

Macaroni au gratin

Apple mosaic tartlets

Dinner for 12 persons

2 SOUPS:

Consommé with rice

Brown purée of turnips

2 FISH:

Brill with lobster sauce

Cod à la provençale

2 REMOVES:

Braised ribs of beef à la mode

Roast sucking pig à l'anglaise

4 ENTRÉES

Scallops of young rabbits in cases with fine herbs

Salmis of partridges with mushrooms.

Chickens with lasagne à l'italienne

Fricandeau with purée of endives

SECOND COURSE

2 ROASTS:

Poulard

Snipes

2 REMOVES:

Croquettes of chestnuts

Pineapple pudding

4 ENTREMETS:

Brussels sprouts dressed with butter

Scalloped mussels au gratin

Puff-paste royals

Apple charlotte

NOVEMBER

Dinner for 8 persons

1 SOUP:
Purée of rabbits à la Chantilly

2 FISH:
Broiled herrings, mustard sauce
Scollops of cod à la hollandaise

2 REMOVES:
Capon with nouilles
Braised neck of mutton larded à la soubise

Calves' brains, fried in batter

2 ENTRÉES:
Kidneys breadcrumbed à la maître d'hôtel
Cutlets of partridges à l'algérienne

SECOND COURSE

2 ROASTS:
Macaroni au gratin
Wild ducks

1 REMOVE:
Orange fritters

4 ENTREMETS:

Celery à la villeroi

Pear cheese à la creme

Poached eggs on anchovy toast

Love's wells garnished with preserve

Dinner for 8 persons

1 SOUP:

Cream of rice à la chasseur

2 FISH:

Fried smelts

Lampreys à la Foley

2 REMOVES:

Goose à la dauphinoise

Fillets of red deer à la royale

Patties au jus

2 ENTRÉES:

Sheeps' tongues à l'écarlate with spinach

Pigeons à la duchesse

SECOND COURSE

2 ROASTS:

Pheasant

Snipes

1 REMOVE:

Pear fritters

4 ENTREMETS:

Salsifis fried in batter

Eggs à la tripe

Rice cake with almonds

Vol-au-vent of apricots

Dinner for 8 persons

1 SOUP:

Purée of lentilles à la soubise

2 FISH:

Fried soles

Tench à la hollandaise

2 REMOVES:

Ham with spinach

Roast turkey à l'anglaise

Bouchées of larks à la Pompadour

2 ENTRÉES:

Fillets of partridges à la Plessy

Scallops of mutton sautées with olives

SECOND COURSE

2 ROASTS:
Russian salad
Widgeon

1 REMOVE:
Vol-au-vent of damsons, with iced cream

4 ENTREMETS:
Eggs à la dauphine
Pomegranate jelly
Endives with cream
Macaroni cake

DECEMBER

Dinner for 6 persons

1 SOUP:

Purée of peas à l'anglaise

1 FISH:

Cod à la crème au gratin

2 REMOVES:

Roast pheasant à la Périgueux

Boiled leg of pork à l'anglaise

2 ENTRÉES:

Blanquette of fowl garnished with potato croquettes

Scallops of beef with oysters

SECOND COURSE

1 ROAST:

Snipes

3 ENTREMETS:

Spinach with poached eggs

Plum pudding

Almond cakes à la Chantilly

Dinner for 6 persons

1 SOUP:
Purée of endives à la crème (preserved)

1 FISH:
Fillets of whitings à la provençale

2 REMOVES:
Snipe pudding à la d'Orsay
Braised pheasant with celery sauce

2 ENTRÉES:
Chickens à la tartare
Mutton cutlets with purée of chestnuts

SECOND COURSE

1 ROAST:
Wild duck

2 ENTREMETS:
Apricot omelette
Apple charlotte
Brussels sprouts with butter

Dinner for 6 persons

1 SOUP:
Consommé with nouilles

1 FISH:
Smelts au gratin

2 REMOVES:
Roast saddle of mutton

Partridges à la soubise

2 ENTRÉES:
Curry of rabbits à l'indienne

Oxtail à la jardinière

SECOND COURSE

1 ROAST:
Larks

3 ENTREMETS:
Potatoes soufflées

Mince pies

Orange jelly à l'anglaise

SUMMER MEALS

Ball Supper for
300 Persons

8 grosses-pièces on ornamental stands:

2 raised pies of fowls and ham with truffles, garnished with jelly

2 hams ornamented with aspic jelly

2 galantines of poulards, with aspic jelly

2 boars' heads, ornamented with aspic jelly

48 cold entrées, dished up on silver plates:

6 groups of plovers' eggs, garnished with aspic jelly

6 lobster salads

6 mayonnaises of fowl

6 plates of cold roast fowls (cut up)

6 mayonnaises of fillets of salmon

6 entrées of lamb-cutlets à la Bellevue

6 plates of tongue, in slices, garnished with aspic jelly

6 entrées of chaud-froid fricassées of chickens

36 cold roast fowls and 4 tongues, to be kept in reserve for the
purpose of replenishing those entrées as they are eaten.

8 grosses-pièces of pastry, on stands:

2 Savoy cakes à la vanille

2 croquantes

2 nougats of almonds and pistachios

1 Baba

1 Victoria cake

16 entremets of small pastry:

cherry tartlets

strawberry and apricot tartlets

fenchonnettes with orange flowers

Genoese cakes with almonds

apricot nougats

florentines

madeleines

duchess loaves

Mecca loaves

Polish cakes

cheesecakes

queen's cakes

small meringues

almond gaufres

puff-paste mosaic tartlets

petits-choux, with pistachios

36 moulds of jellies and creams:

6 currant jellies, garnished with peaches

6 pineapple jellies

6 cherry jellies

6 macédoine jellies

6 Russian charlottes

6 strawberry charlottes

3 soups, to be served from the buffet:

spring soup

Vermicelli clear soup

purée of fowls or cream of barley

24 hot roast fowls

French beans, new potatoes

Glossary of British Culinary Terms

The following glossary and conversion tables should be of use to those aspiring chefs who wish to reproduce the dishes in this book.

Due to the impact of French cuisine, much of the food eaten in the royal establishment is described in French, even though many of the dishes do have equivalent English names. However, the royal cooks have always attempted to ensure that everybody is talking the same language – even if it isn't always English – which is particularly essential for grander occasions, when many assistant chefs are required. Like every art form, cooking has its own vocabulary, and as knowledge and skills are passed from one generation to the next, it clearly helps if the interpretation remains the same.

Of course, all the recipes were created at a time when the standard form of weights and measures was imperial and not all of these concepts remained the same after they were converted to the metric system.

AUBERGINE: Eggplant.

BARD (to bard a fillet): To wrap a fillet or other lean meat in bacon or sheet pork fat. The fat will melt during cooking and keep the meat from drying out.

BARLEY WATER: A traditional, refreshing cold drink made from water and a boiled barley mixture, usually flavoured with lemon or orange juice and perhaps a little sugar. A pitcher of barley water was carried to people working in the fields, or served like lemonade.

BÉCHAMEL: A rich white sauce made with milk infused with herbs and other flavourings.

BITTER ALMONDS: If not available, use almond extract for similar results.

BLACK TREACLE: Black molasses.

BLANCHED ALMONDS: Almonds that have had the brown inner skin removed by scorching. (To blanch, pour boiling water over the almonds and allow to stand for 3-5 minutes, after which the skin will slide off. Keep the almonds in hot water until you are ready to peel them, taking out only a few at a time. If the water cools and the brown skin hardens, repeat the process.)

BLOATERS: Herring cured by salting and smoking.

BLOND OF VEAL: The juices and fat trickling from veal roast.

CASTOR SUGAR: Finely granulated white or pale golden sugar.

CLARIFIED: Applies to butter and fats that have been heated in order to separate out the impurities. The fat is strained and the solids thrown away to leave a clear fat. Fat treated this way will brown foods evenly without brown spots and will heat to higher temperatures than ordinary butter without burning, which is why it is used in fine cooking. It also keeps for some time without refrigeration. Ghee, the fat used in Indian cooking, is butter treated this way.

CODDLED: Food, especially eggs, cooked in water just below boiling point.

COMFITS: Preserved sugared fruit, such as apricots, plums, orange slices, marrons, and so on.

CORN: Wheat, grain in general.

CORNFLOWER: Cornstarch.

COURGETTES: Zucchini squash.

CREAM OF RICE: Rice ground as finely as flour. Used for thickening and for puddings.

DOUBLE CREAM: Heavy cream.

DOUBLE SAUCEPAN: Double boiler.

DRIPPING: The fat and juices that drip from meat being roasted. Used for gravies, sauces and cooking in general.

EN COCOTTE: Individual portions of food cooked (mostly in the oven) in small round or oblong heatproof casseroles. Cocotte is a French word for casserole.

FORCEMEAT: A mixture of meat or vegetables chopped and seasoned for use as a stuffing or garnish.

FUMET: A concentrated stock, especially of game or fish, used as flavouring. Fumet of duck would be made by boiling the bones and less attractive parts of the bird with herbs, and so on, then straining it prior to further use.

GOLDEN SYRUP: A sweet, golden syrup related to molasses, used for flavouring puddings. There is no American equivalent; honey and maple syrup can be used, though the flavour of the dish will be different. However, golden syrup is sold in gourmet shops specialising in imported foods.

GROUNDNUT OIL: Peanut oil.

ICING SUGAR: Confectioners' sugar.

KIDNEY SOUP: An old-fashioned soup containing kidneys. A great Victorian favourite.

KIPPER: A fish cured by salting and drying or smoking, especially herring. Kippers are standard and beloved English breakfast fare.

KIRSCHWASSER: Kirsch. A dry, white, potent spirit distilled from the fermented juice of cherries in Germany, France and Switzerland.

LARD: to lard a fillet To thread strips of bacon or sheet lard into a lean piece of meat to make it juicier or to flavour it. Special larding needles, or 'lardoons', can be inserted into the meat with a skewer or a knitting needle.

LEMON CURD: A conserve with a thick consistency made from lemons, sugar, butter and eggs. Used to fill tarts or to spread on toast.

LINED 9-INCH TIN: Nine-inch cake pan greased and lined with waxed or unglazed brown paper.

MAIZE: Corn meal.

MORELLO: A dark red, almost black sweet-sour cherry ideally suited for cooking.

MUSLIN: Cheesecloth used for straining.

NOUILLES PASTE: Noodle dough.

PEEL: Glacé orange, lemon, or citron peel

PLAIN CHOCOLATE: Sweet cooking chocolate.

PLAIN FLOUR: All-purpose flour.

POUNDED SUGAR: This term, found in old recipes, goes back to the days when sugar was sold in cones wrapped in blue paper. Pieces had to be chipped off the cones, and in order to get smooth sugar, the sugar pieces were pounded using a pestle and mortar.

POWDERED YEAST: Granulated yeast.

PRAWNS: A small saltwater crayfish. Medium and large shrimps are the nearest equivalent. In England, shrimps are tiny.

QUENELLE: A dumpling made with a spiced fish or meat forcemeat bound with fat and eggs; it is then moulded into a small sausage or egg shape and poached in boiling water.

RASHER: A thin slice of bacon or ham.

RISSOLE: Small ball of ground meat, fish or eggs mixed with spices, coated in bread crumbs, or covered with pastry, and sautéed.

SAGO FLOUR: A starch prepared from certain palm trees, used for making desserts and much used in Victorian cookery.

SAVOURIES: Non-sweet, tasty and often piquant dishes eaten in small quantities after the dessert to clear the palate for the port, Madeira and brandy to come. For all intents and purposes, savouries make fine hors d'oeuvres and appetizers as well as main dishes for suppers and lunches.

SAVOY CAKE: Sponge cake.

SELF-RAISING FLOUR: Flour with baking powder added to it.

SEMOLINA: Coarse wheat flour, used in puddings and in pasta. Cream of wheat is the nearest equivalent, but real semolina

can be found in Middle Eastern groceries, since it is a staple in those countries.

SHALLOT: A bulb that resembles a cross between an onion and garlic and tastes that way. Used for fine cooking.

STREAKY BACON: Lean bacon.

TAMMY: Strainer.

THICK SOUP, CLEAR SOUP: The first was a cream or gravy soup, the second consommé. Formal, old-fashioned English dinners included both, and each diner would be asked their preference.

THIN CREAM: Coffee cream.

VANILLA POD: Vanilla bean.

VANILLA SUGAR: Confectioners' or super-fine sugar flavoured with vanilla bean. Used to flavour bakings, desserts and fruit. (Can be kept indefinitely in an airtight container.)

VEAL FILLET: Best-quality boneless veal.

VEGETABLE STOCK: Stock made from vegetables rather than meat.

WHITE GLACÉ ICING: Smooth, hard icing made with icing sugar and water.

WHITE STOCK: Stock made from veal and chicken bones and deliberately kept light in colour. Used for soups, sauces, and so on.

WOODCOCK: A European game bird related to the snipe, with a long bill and short legs. A favourite bird for both hunters and gourmets alike.

Recipe Index

Compote of Dried Figs 189
Compote of Fruit 176
Consommé aux Quenelles 42
Consommé Cyrano 44
Consommé Tomate Froid 43
Cote de Veau Sauté Chasseur 107
Cotelettes d'Agneau 117
Cotelettes d'Agneau sur le Grille 119
Cottage Pie de Boeuf Braisé 121
Crabe Sauce Rémoulade 100
Cream of Pea Soup 38
Cream of Pearl Barley à la Victoria 47
Cream of Rice à la Cardinal 47
Cream of Rice à la Royale 48
Cream of Rice à la Victoria 49
Crème au Caramel 184
Crème Brûlée 175
Crème de Céleri 43
Crèpes Suzettes 172
Croquettes de Canard Sauvage 156
Croquettes de Gibier 153
Currant Buns 27
Curry de Poulet 135

Délice de Sole d'Antin 85
Dinde Rôtie Palace 143

Eclairs au Café 30
Eggs à la Tripe 16
Eggs au Gratin 17
Escalopes de Veau Viennoise 105
Eton Mess aux Framboises 179

Faisan en Casserole 156
Faisans Poêlés aux Céleris Sauce Suprême 145
Filet de Boeuf Montmorency 125
Filet de Merluche Saint-Germain 77
Filet de Sole Frits 87
Filet de Sole Veronique 78
Foie de Veau Sauté au Lard 107
Fried Egg and Bacon 10

Gelée de Gibier 155

Ginger Cake 22
Goujonettes de Merlans Sauce Tartare 90
Goujonettes de Sole 80
Grilled Chicken 135
Grouse a la Crème 144

Haddocks à la Royale 98
Hare Soup à la St George 49
Haricots Verts à la Crème 162
Haricots Verts Sauté au Beurre 166
Herrings Fried in Oatmeal 102
Homard à l'Americaine 103

Irish Stew 116

La Quiche Lorraine (traditional) 67
Laitues Braisés au Jus 165
Lemon Curd Sponge 27
Loin of Veal à la Royale 113

Macaroni au Gratin 69
Macaroni Soup à la Royale 58
Macédoine de Fruits 179
Marrow Toast 73
Mayonnaise de Homard 104
Mayonnaise of Fillets of Soles 75
Merlans à la Meunière 91
Merlans Colbert 91
Millefeuilles aux Pommes 182
Mince Meat à la Royale 76
Mincemeat Puffs 23
Mushrooms à la Crème 68
Mushrooms Sautéd in Butter 67
Mutton Pies 129

Navarin d'Agneau aux Legumes 117
Neck of Veal à la Royale 109
Noix or Cushion of Veal à la St George 112
Nutritious Liquid Custard of Chicken 46
Nutritious Liquid Custard of Game 60

Oeufs Brouillés Meyerbeer 10
Oeufs en Cocotte a la Crème with

This book is dedicated to all the people who
helped keep a small corner of history alive and made
it possible for the contents of this book finally to
be published. It is also dedicated to my friends
Gus & Sheila Dudgeon, whose friendship, support
and enthusiasm I will always remember.

PAUL FISHMAN